Barbara Hehner

THE TUNNEL KING

The True Story of Wally Floody
and the Great Escape

Harper*Trophy*Canada™
An imprint of HarperCollins*PublishersLtd*

The Tunnel King
© 2004 by Barbara Hehner.
All rights reserved.

Published by HarperTrophyCanada™,
an imprint of HarperCollins Publishers Ltd

No part of this book may be used or reproduced
in any manner whatsoever without the prior
written permission of the publisher, except in
the case of brief quotations embodied in reviews.

HarperTrophyCanada™ is a trademark of
HarperCollins Publishers

First Edition

HarperCollins books may be purchased for
educational, business, or sales promotional use
through our Special Markets Department.

HarperCollins Publishers Ltd
2 Bloor Street East, 20th Floor
Toronto, Ontario, Canada
M4W 1A8

www.harpercollins.ca

Library and Archives Canada Cataloguing in
Publication

Hehner, Barbara, 1947–
The tunnel king : the true story of Wally
Floody and the great escape / Barbara
Hehner.

ISBN 0–00–639477–9

1. Floody, Wally – Juvenile literature.
2. Stalag Luft III – Juvenile literature.
3. Escapes – Poland – Żagań – Juvenile
literature. 4. World War, 1939–1945 –
Prisoners and prisons, German – Juvenile
literature. 5. Canada. Royal Canadian Air
Force – Biography – Juvenile literature.
6. Prisoners of war – Canada – Biography –
Juvenile literature. 7. Mining engineers –
Canada – Biography – Juvenile literature.
I. Title.

D805.G3H45 2004   j940.54´7243´092
C2004-903139-2

RRD 9 8 7 6 5 4 3

Printed and bound in the United States
Set in Ehrhardt

THE TUNNEL KING

To Eric

CONTENTS

CENTRAL EUROPE

DENMARK

North Sea

• Flensburg

Lübeck •

Hamburg •

E L B E

NETHERLANDS

W E S E R

Alkmaar •

G E R M M

• Amsterdam
• Utrecht

Kassel •

• Spangenberg

RHINE

Antwerp •

Cologne •

DULAG-LUFT

St. Omer •

BELGIUM

Brussels •

Frankfurt •
am Main

Nuremberg •

SEINE

• Paris

Saarbrücken •

Ettlingen •

Strasbourg •

Stühlingen •

Dachau •

Munich

F R A N C E

Mulhouse •

Schaffhausen •

Berchtesgaden

Bodensee

Basel •

• Zürich

• Bern

SWITZERLAND

Geneva •

I T

CAVE IN!

Wally Floody lay on his side, propped up painfully on one elbow. He was in a 2-foot-square space, so cramped that he could not turn around. His only light came from a small tin filled with melted margarine and a wick made from pyjama cord. The lamp flickered and stank, and coated his mouth and throat with oily soot. But the lamp had to stay. Even the bravest tunneller could not bear the thought of working in complete darkness.

Behind Wally were 20 feet of tunnel, shored up (reinforced) with boards to keep the walls and ceiling from collapsing. Just above his head was unshored sand— tons of it. But the veteran tunneller wouldn't let himself think about that. Instead, he concentrated on the wall of yellow sand just in front of his face. He hacked at it with his knife, then pushed the sand back to Hank Birkland, his digging partner. Hank picked up the sand with a scoop cut from a milk can. When his wooden box was full, Hank tugged on the rope tied to the box. Two men waiting at the tunnel mouth hauled the box back.

Wally heard a hissing sound just above his ear, as if a snake was dangling there. He knew what it was and backed up frantically. Behind him, Hank was also scrambling. Then, wet and cold and stinking, the roof came down on Wally. He tried to hold a little space around his face with his hands, but in seconds the sand was packing his nostrils and his mouth. He felt someone tugging on his legs and then he blacked out.

When Wally came to, gagging and spluttering, he was in the room carved out at the mouth of the tunnel. The men who manned the air pump and packed the sand in bags were looking on with concern. Hank and Wally stared at each other. They saw the filthy, torn longjohns both of them were wearing, their matted hair sticking in all directions, their eyes round and panicked in their grimy faces—and started to laugh.

Flight Lieutenant Wally Floody was 25 years old, with dark hair and hazel eyes. He had been tall and lean to begin with. Prisoner-of-war rations, combined with the hard labour of digging tunnels, had left him gaunt and hollow-eyed. He had been buried alive several times before this and had felt the terror of suffocation. Once the lamp had spilled hot oil against his thigh as the roof caved in, so he had been burned as well as choked. But by 1943, he had been a prisoner of war in Germany for two years, and he wanted more than anything to escape. The best way out of Stalag Luft III, a prison camp for airmen, seemed to be a tunnel under the barbed-wire fence. Wally knew how to build tunnels—so he would go back down tomorrow, and the next day, and he would keep digging.

Chapter 1

LOOKING FOR ADVENTURE

Clarke Wallace Chant Floody was born in Chatham, Ontario, on April 28, 1918. When he was a year old, his family moved to Toronto, where Wally's father, William Edward, went to work in magazine publishing. Wally's younger sister, Catherine, was born soon after the move.

As he grew up, Wally was always the tallest boy in his class. His long arms and legs were thin, even though he had a hearty appetite. His mother believed he burned off everything he ate because he was rarely still. In the summers, he went to a sleep-over camp on the Toronto Islands. He also spent part of each summer on a farm in Clinton, Ontario, where his mother had relatives. He helped to look after the livestock and he learned to ride a horse. However, he always returned to Toronto in time for the "Ex," the Canadian National Exhibition. His Clinton cousins often came with him.

*Wally, about age nine,
as an Anglican Church choir boy.*

On Young Canada Day at the exhibition, admission for kids was free and the rides and games cost only a nickel apiece. Wally, Catherine and their cousins joined thousands of other children swarming through the Princes' Gates. First, they headed for the Pure Food Building, where they could stuff themselves with free food samples. Then it was over to the midway. No matter how high the Ferris wheel climbed, or how fast the roller coaster dropped, Wally always wished they went higher and faster.

Wally began high school at Northern Vocational in

the fall of 1932. By grade 11, he was well over 6 feet tall, and active in team sports, especially basketball and football. As one of the junior football team's starting halfbacks, Wally had his picture taken by a newspaper photographer. It was an exciting day in the Floody house when the picture was published, and Catherine pasted it in her scrapbook. As soon as the football season ended, basketball practice began. Wally was the starting centre on Northern's junior basketball team, and its second leading scorer.

In 1935, Wally was in grade 12 and old enough to join

Wally at age 16, playing football for Northern Vocational School.

Northern's senior teams. The Northern senior football team took the city championship that year. Wally played in the championship game at Varsity Stadium, the biggest stadium in the city. Nearly 10,000 people came to watch, including sports reporters from all three Toronto newspapers. The next day, Northern students paraded through the school neighbourhood, carrying Wally and the other football heroes on their shoulders.

Although Wally loved playing sports, he was bored and restless in class. By springtime of grade 12, he wanted to leave school. His marks were slipping badly. Besides, in 1936 Canada was suffering through the Great Depression. Many people all across the country had lost their jobs. Wally's father was still working, but he was not making as much money as he used to. Wally was now 18 years old. If he could find a job, he could help out with the family's income.

Through his father's contacts in the publishing business, Wally got a job selling advertising for the *Toronto Star*. But he missed being outdoors, and he missed being able to play sports. Then he heard about a job that sounded much more exciting than selling ads—and it paid better, too. The gold mines in Northern Ontario were hiring young men who were good athletes. Not only would they be given jobs in the mines, but they would also get to play on company sports teams. Games in the intermine leagues were hotly contested, and mine owners competed with each other to sign up the best players they could find.

In June of 1936, Wally got on a train and headed north. That summer, he worked at the Preston East Dome Mine in Timmins, Ontario. He played baseball on the company team, though it was not his best sport. He spent the fall and winter back at his job with the *Toronto Star*, but in May of 1937, he headed north once again. This time he went to Kirkland Lake, and took a job with the Lake Shore Mines.

Wally worked as a mucker, shovelling the mud and rock that had been blasted out of the ground, and loading it into carts so it could be hauled up to the surface. A person needed strong muscles to be a mucker and Wally was strong. It was hard work, but it paid pretty well. Wally made $4.75 per day.

Dressed in denim overalls and a workshirt, steel-toed boots and a hard helmet, Wally reported for work at the top of the mineshaft five or six days a week. Lake Shore Mines was one of the largest gold mines in the world, and during the years of the Depression, the miners worked in shifts around the clock. Wally might start work at seven in the morning, three in the afternoon, or eleven o'clock at night.

No matter what time the shift started, the workday began the same way—by checking the big board. Wally would remove one of the two tags that hung on the board below his name. Everyone had to do this. It was

Wally in miner's overalls and helmet, Kirkland Lake.

the best and simplest way to tell who was working where. One tag under your name meant you were underground. Two tags meant you were on the surface.

Next came the elevator ride down the shaft. The metal cage, carrying 20 standing men, rocked and swayed as it made its way down, thousands of feet into the earth. Even with his helmet light on, Wally felt as if the intense darkness of the mine was pressing down on him. In time he got used to it, just as he learned to endure the choking dust from all the digging and blasting.

Wally sometimes found himself in places where there wasn't enough room for him to stand up straight.

However, the biggest passageways were more than high enough to stand in, and they had trolley tracks to move the muckers' carts. They were also shored up with wooden beams and boards to keep the walls and roof from caving in on the miners. A rockburst could kill a man in an instant, or trap him under the ground for days. Mine workers had to learn not to think about that.

Once basketball practice began in October, the company gave Wally work above ground, where his fingers were less likely to be crushed. Wally was one of several new basketball players hired to play for the Lake Shore team, called the Blue Devils. He was not one of the team's top scorers, but with his height, he was able to grab plenty of rebounds and be a strong defensive player.

The Blue Devils finished the season in first place, then had to take on the second-place team in the league championship series. In the final game— a tough, bruising match against the team from the Wright-Hargreaves mine—Wally scored a key basket to help his team to the Mines League Championship and the Carling Cup. A few days later, the Blue Devils travelled to North Bay to play for the championship of all Northern Ontario. The largest crowd ever to attend a basketball game in North Bay watched the Lake Shore Blue Devils beat their hometown team.

* * *

Wally returned to Toronto in September 1938 and went back to work as an advertising salesman. One night early in December, Wally got a telephone call from a friend he knew from Kirkland Lake.

"There's a bunch of us in town for a few days," he told Wally, "and we've got an extra ticket for the big game on Saturday. Thought you might be interested."

This was certainly a piece of luck. Wally had been hoping to get a ticket, and the 1938 Grey Cup game turned out to be a thriller. The Winnipeg Blue Bombers were leading 7–6 after the third quarter, but in the last 15 minutes, the Toronto Argonauts scored four touchdowns (worth five points each at the time, plus four points for the conversions), to win the game 30–7.

For Wally, something else made the game even more memorable. His friends introduced him to a young woman named Betty Baxter. Betty was from St. Catharines, but she was working in Toronto. Her grandfather had owned a mine in Kirkland Lake and she had spent part of her childhood there. Wally was attracted to Betty right away. He thought she was smart, funny and beautiful. Within a few months of the Grey Cup game, they were talking about getting married. But there was something else Wally wanted to do first.

Wally and a friend named Ches were planning to take a trip around North America by riding the rails. Many men, out of work or with little money, travelled this way during the Depression years of the 1930s. You ran alongside a moving freight train as it slowly left a station, then you hauled yourself into an empty freight car. Before the train reached its destination, you had to jump out while it was still moving. It was a dangerous way to travel, and not just because you might get hurt. If you got caught riding the trains this way, the "bulls" (railroad security men armed with clubs) might beat you up.

Wally had a feeling that if he and Ches didn't take their trip now, there might not be another chance. By the end of 1938, it was plain to everyone that Canada could soon be involved in a war. Newspaper headlines were becoming more and more ominous. Japan was invading neighbouring countries in Asia. There was also trouble in Europe. In Germany, dictator Adolf Hitler had taken control of the country. Hitler's Nazi party was viciously anti-Semitic, and had begun to terrorize Jews and send them to concentration camps. The Nazis were also building up Germany's military might. They had already taken over Austria and part of Czechoslovakia. By March of 1939, they would occupy the rest. If Britain was drawn into war in Europe, Canada, as part of the British Commonwealth, would likely go to war, too. And if it did, able-bodied young men like Wally would be expected to fight.

Wally and Ches left on their journey in the spring of 1939. They got all the way down to Mexico and then began to make their way back north. Whenever they ran low on money, they would stop somewhere and find work. For a while, they got jobs as carnies in a travelling carnival, helping to move and set up tents, and selling tickets on the midway. It turned out that some of the games on the midway were fixed—no matter how many balls you threw at the milk bottles, they were never all going to fall over. Wally and Ches only found out about that when angry townsfolk in Joplin, Missouri, confronted the owners of the carnival. They threatened to smash up the midway and throw everyone in jail if the carnies weren't out of town by suppertime. It was Wally's 21st birthday. As he and Ches jumped a freight car out of town, Wally thought it might be the worst birthday he would ever have.

Wally and Ches stayed away from carnival work after that. They managed to get jobs as cowboys instead, taking the lowliest, dustiest, smelliest job of riding behind the herd. Back in Canada that summer, they worked in a lumber camp at first, then went to Alberta to seek work as cowboys again. They wouldn't be there long.

Chapter 2

SIGNING UP

On September 1, 1939, Germany invaded Poland. Britain, which had promised to protect Poland, declared war on Germany on September 3. Canada declared war on Germany one week later. This was the beginning of the Second World War, a conflict that would eventually reach into the lives of almost everyone on earth. On one side were the Axis powers—including Germany, Italy and later Japan. On the other side were the Allies, which included Britain and the Commonwealth countries such as Canada and Australia, and later the Soviet Union and the United States. The war would be longer and more terrible than anyone could imagine when it began.

On the day Canada declared war, Wally and Ches were working on a ranch in Empress, Alberta. Wally had already made up his mind that if war came, he was going to join the Royal Canadian Air Force (RCAF). He thought that with his strength, speed and coordination, he would make a good fighter pilot.

Wally wanted to return to Toronto right away, but he didn't have enough money for the train fare. He paid his way home by shovelling coal into the boiler of the locomotive, for the entire trip back to Toronto. The very next day, he went downtown to the RCAF Recruiting Depot.

Wally filled out an application there. He had come armed with a letter of recommendation from his high school principal. Wally knew that to get into the RCAF, he was supposed to have junior matriculation (the completion of grade 12), and he didn't quite have that. However, his principal had written a glowing letter, saying that Wally was a fine young man and that his various courses actually added up to the equivalent of matriculation. The recruiting office told Wally that he appeared qualified, but they couldn't accept him just yet. While Wally was ready for the air force, the air force wasn't ready for him.

When war broke out, the Allied forces had very few combat aircraft. They had even fewer military pilots. Britain, Canada, Australia and New Zealand agreed to join in the British Commonwealth Air Training Plan (BCATP). Most of the training would take place in Canada, which had wide open spaces, especially on the Prairies, and was far from the fighting. At first, the instructors would be bush pilots, stunt pilots known as

*Posters such as this encouraged patriotic
young Canadians like Wally to join the RCAF.*

"barnstormers," crop-dusters and a few veteran airmen who had fought in World War I, over 20 years earlier. Most of their students would be sent into the war, but some of the best pilots would be kept in Canada, where they were needed as instructors.

At its peak, the BCATP would turn out 3,000 graduates a month, at more than 200 sites across Canada. In all, the Plan would train more than 130,000 aircrew in less than five years. But in the fall of 1939, when Wally tried to join up, the RCAF was still scrambling to find instructors and to set up training schools for pilots and other aircrew. The recruiting officer could only assure a disappointed Wally that the air force would get back to him. Through the winter Wally stayed in Toronto, taking odd jobs and playing for a local basketball team.

It was an uneasy time. Even though the nations of Europe had now declared war on each other, neither side launched any large attacks. People called this time "the Phony War." It ended dramatically in May 1940, when Germany invaded and overran Belgium, the Netherlands and Luxembourg. Within days they had also invaded France. Each time, their tactics were the same: a sudden, overwhelming air attack by the Luftwaffe (the German air force), followed by an invasion of ground troops. They called it *Blitzkrieg* (lightning war), and so far no country had withstood it. After France fell, Britain seemed to be the next logical target. To reach the British Isles, though, German troops would have to cross the English Channel by boat. They could not do that safely until Germany first got control of British airspace. To save themselves from invasion, the British knew they would have to fight off the Luftwaffe.

More than ever, Wally wanted to get into the air force and go overseas to help the RAF (Britain's Royal Air Force), but the RCAF still hadn't notified him to report for training. In the midst of this uncertainty, Wally and Betty went ahead with their plan to get married on May 24, 1940. They moved north to Kirkland

Lake so that Wally could go back to working in the mines while he waited to be called up. Meanwhile, other men Wally knew were beginning their flying training. He was getting impatient. Why hadn't he heard from the RCAF?

On Thanksgiving weekend of 1940, Wally and Betty were in Toronto, visiting family. Wally decided to stop in at the downtown Recruiting Depot to see what was going on. He learned that single men were being taken for the air force first. His application had been moved to the bottom of the pile because he was now married.

"What's that got to do with it?" Wally said indignantly. "My wife backs me in this 100 per cent."

The recruiting officer relented. He told Wally that there was a train leaving Union Station that very evening. If he got to it in time, he'd be on his way to the Manning Depot in Brandon, Manitoba, the first step in his air force career. Wally rushed home to pack and say a quick goodbye to his family.

Number 2 Manning Depot in Brandon, Manitoba, was housed in a huge building with high ceilings and a concrete floor, known as the Cow Palace. Before the war it had been used for agricultural exhibitions, and there was still a strong aroma of cattle and horses in the air. Now it was home to more than 2,000 young men who wanted to be in the RCAF. Some of them would be sent on for further air training; others would be sent to ground school to learn various trades that would keep aircraft and air fields operational. Wally wanted only to fly.

In Brandon, Wally was thrown into military life right away. Like the other recruits, he was now an Aircraftsman 2—an "Acey-deucy," as they were dubbed, the lowest of the low in the air force. He would earn $1.30 a day.

On his first night, Wally had a hard time falling asleep. Partly it was excitement. Partly it was the strangeness of sleeping in a metal-frame lower bunk with a complete stranger snoring a couple of inches above his head. All around him were hundreds of other young men he didn't know, tossing, turning, muttering in their sleep. Wally didn't realize it yet, but training was going to be so exhausting that he would never have trouble sleeping again.

The next morning, Wally was given a sheet of paper with 70 different steps on it. He was supposed to follow all of them. Each one had to be initialled by an officer. Each one of them involved a long lineup. Wally was issued with boots and uniforms (the first ones he got were too small for him), including the RCAF wedge cap, which he learned to put on his head at a jaunty angle. He was also issued with almost everything else the air force thought he would need, including something called a "housewife." This little leather case contained supplies for polishing boots and buttons, and a needle and thread for mending.

The most uncomfortable lineup was for the medical inspection. Wally had to stand naked with a whole lot of other men while doctors examined them. He got so many injections at the Manning Depot that for a few days his arm felt like a lead weight hanging from his shoulder. He filled out many forms that asked his name, age, education, work experience, religion, next of kin . . . He took his turn at latrine duty (cleaning the bathroom), and at kitchen duty (peeling potatoes). He learned to march, often "on the double," which was almost a run. And he learned when and how to salute. There was a saying around the Manning Depot, "If it's on the ground, pick it up. If you can't pick it up, paint over it. If you can't paint over it, salute it."

Wally toughed it out for a month. Then, in the middle of November, he got the word he had been waiting for. He was ordered to report to No. 2 Initial Training School (ITS) in Regina, Saskatchewan. His serious air training was about to begin.

Chapter 3

GETTING WINGS

Wally stood outside the Link trainer room, waiting his turn. He hadn't been in a Link yet, but he knew what it was. It was a machine that tested your flying ability without risking your life. If you made a mistake on a training flight, you might crash, but if you made a mistake on the Link, you were still safe on the ground. Still, Wally was nervous. If he messed up on the Link, he could lose his chance to train as a pilot.

An aircraftsman came out the door on wobbly legs. His face was pale and sweaty. "It's just like the real thing, all right," he said to Wally. Then he clapped his hands over his mouth and scurried toward the exit. Wally tried to stay calm. He reminded himself of how rock-steady his stomach had always been on roller coasters. He could do this!

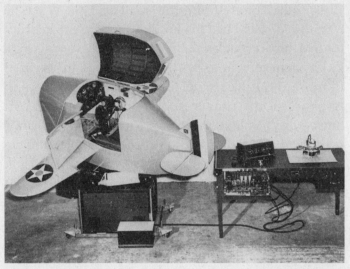

The Link trainer was the first flight simulator. The Link was designed in 1930 by an American pilot, Ed Link, to make air training safer. Before the Link, the only way to learn to fly was in the air, being instructed by another pilot. This was both expensive and dangerous.

Wally went inside and reported to the Link instructor. The instructor sat at a desk cluttered with radio equipment and recording devices. Wires ran from the desk to a raised platform in the middle of the room, where the Link trainer waited. The Link looked to Wally like an airplane in a cartoon: it had a fat little body with a pair of stubby wings jutting out from it.

Wally folded himself into the small cockpit. When he was settled in and had his headphones on, the instructor took him through a flight drill.

A system of bellows with compressed air was used to move the Link trainer up, down and sideways in response to the rudder pedals and the control column. For 20 minutes, as his instructor issued commands on the radio, Wally made the Link simulate banking, climbing and diving. He even put the Link into a simulated spin and then pulled out of it. He felt completely focused on what he was doing, and didn't notice how tense he had become until the test was over. His hands had gripped the control wheel so tightly that his fingers were cramped.

Wally left the room happy and excited. "Piece of cake!" he said to the next guy waiting.

At the end of the five-week ITS course, some men would be sent home. Only the best would be chosen to continue with air force training. Some would train as fighter pilots, learning to fly alone in single-engine planes. Some would train as bomber pilots, who would one day fly with a co-pilot and other crew members in two- and four-engine planes. Others would become air gunners, wireless (radio) operators, or air observers (navigators) on bombers. Wally was determined to be a fighter pilot.

For much of the day, Wally was back in a classroom. This time he had no intention of dropping out. So, even though his days started at 6:00 a.m., some nights he was up until midnight reading textbooks and doing assignments. He studied Mathematics, Navigation, Wireless (radio), Armaments, Air Force Law and other subjects. Between classes, the students were herded outside for PT (physical training). For Wally, who had always kept in shape, this was the easiest part of the day. And of course, there was parade drill—marching, marching and more marching. Wally couldn't quite see the point—when he got into the war, he would be doing his fighting in the air. But it was all part of military discipline. He was now Leading Aircraftsman Floody, earning $1.50 a day.

Finally, it was Selection Day. Each member of the class would have one last chance to make a good impression before a panel of instructors and senior air force officers. Wally knew he stood about midpoint in the class. Would they send him on for pilot training? His name was called: "LAC Floody, Wallace."

Wally cleared his throat and walked in to face the panel.

"You want to be a pilot?" barked one grey-haired officer with a chestful of medals.

"Yes, sir."

"What special abilities do you have to be a pilot?"

"Well, sir, I have excellent hand-eye coordination . . ."

The rest of the interview passed in a blur. But he

must have said the right things. The next day, Wally learned that he was going back to Ontario, to the Elementary Flying Training School in Port Hope.

At long last, Wally was going to get airborne. He was issued with a flight suit and gauntlets (gloves), fleece-lined boots, goggles and a helmet. His first flights at Port Hope were in a plane called a Fleet Finch II. It had a 125 horsepower engine and a maximum speed of 103 miles per hour. The Fleet Finch II looked a lot like planes Wally had seen as a boy in the 1920s. It was a biplane with dual controls. The student sat in the front seat, and the flight instructor sat behind him. They communicated over the roar of the engines using speaking tubes and earphones in their helmets. The cockpit was unheated, and it was January. Wally layered on as much clothing as would fit under his flight suit to try to stay warm. It was hard to have the light touch needed for the Fleet's controls when your hands were stiff with cold.

After eight hours of dual flying time, practising "circuits and bumps" (takeoffs and landings), Wally was judged ready to make his first solo flight on January 11, 1941. He had to take off into the wind, climb to 1,000 feet crosswind, fly downwind, descend to 500 feet, turn back into the wind, throttle back to slow the plane to a landing speed and bring the plane down safely "on the button" (at the near end of the landing strip).

Wally had watched other student pilots on their first flights, and he knew all the mistakes that could happen. Some came in too high and had to go around again. Others ground-looped as they landed, losing control of the airplane and spinning around. Some unlucky ones even crashed. Wally never forgot the exhilaration he felt when he brought his plane down safely for the first time. But that was just the beginning.

Wally's class at the RCAF Elementary Flying School in Port Hope. Wally is standing on the left end.

Wally learned to put the aircraft into a spin and recover from it, and to make it do loops and slow rolls. Instrument flying was another challenge. The cockpit of Wally's plane was covered with a hood to simulate flying in thick clouds or at night. With his view blocked, he had to rely on the dials on his control panel to fly. The instructor was in the back seat to correct any mistakes. Wally practised instrument flying in the Link trainer as well, with the lid of the cockpit closed so that it was completely dark. After 20 hours of flying time, and again at 50 hours, there were flight tests. Each time, some of the students were sent home or to training schools for other aircrew. Wally made it through all these hurdles. On March 6, 1941, he moved on to the final stage of getting his pilot's wings: the Service Flying Training School in Dunnville, Ontario.

Now Wally was a fighter pilot in training, flying two-seater, single-engine Harvards. These planes were painted bright yellow to make student pilots as visible as possible in the sky. Harvards were much faster, at over 200 miles per hour, and much more powerful, at 600 horsepower, than the Fleet Finches Wally had flown before. He practised climbing, steep turns, stalling and recovering at various altitudes, taking off into the wind and low-level flying. Later he added night

*Four North American Harvards
flying in formation near Ottawa, July 1941.*

landings, formation flying and aerobatics—loops, rolls and spins.

Wally's instructors wanted to give him the most thorough training they could, in the short time they had available. They pushed him to repeat every drill until it became second nature. At the same time, the instructors were well aware that Wally and the others would soon be in combat. Their students needed confidence, even daring—these were the things that might keep them alive in aerial battles. Some student airmen at Dunnville tried stunts that were officially forbidden. Several of them flew under the Rainbow Bridge, which was almost finished, but not yet open to traffic, at Niagara Falls.

The final weeks of training were a dangerous time for a young pilot like Wally. During the years of the British Commonwealth Air Training Plan, 47 airmen were killed in flying accidents at Dunnville. Only 11 of these deaths were the result of unauthorized low-level flying or aerobatics. The rest came about from the combination of inexperienced pilots and the necessity of training them in risky manoeuvres. By April 22, Wally had 110 hours of flying time. He had had some close calls, but no accidents. He passed his final, most gruelling flight test, known as the Wings Test, at the end of April. With a flight instructor in the back seat giving him orders, Wally had to perform, coolly and correctly, every flying skill he was asked to demonstrate.

Saturday, May 17, was graduation day for Wally's class of 46 pilots. With Betty, Catherine and his parents looking on, Wally marched smartly up to his commanding officer and had his wings pinned to the chest of his uniform. He was now Pilot Officer Floody. He had a pay raise to $4.25 a day—still a little less than he had made as a teenaged mucker in the gold mines.

These were exciting times for both Wally and Betty, and she would always remember the frantic pace of the

Wally and Betty around the time
he got his wings in May 1941.

next few days. With other graduates from Wally's class, they went to the Park Plaza Hotel in Toronto for an evening of dining and dancing. The next night it was Betty's birthday, and they celebrated again. They also made the rounds of their relatives in Southern Ontario, so that Wally could say goodbye. Then Betty travelled with Wally by train to Halifax, Nova Scotia, to see him off. He was to board a ship for England on May 26. Before Betty really had time to be sad or frightened about what was happening, Wally was gone. It would be more than four years before Betty saw her husband again.

Chapter 4

401 SQUADRON

Wally travelled to England on a crowded passenger liner that had been converted to a troop carrier. Because of the constant danger of attack by "wolf-packs" of German U-boats (submarines), Allied ships crossed the Atlantic in large convoys, guarded by destroyers and corvettes. It was a slow journey because the convoy could travel only at the speed of the slowest ship. And it was nerve-wracking. A torpedo fired from a U-boat could bring disaster at any hour of the day or night. When Wally looked into the sea, he could see planks, boxes, lifebelts and empty lifeboats—the floating wreckage from previous convoys.

A few days after they left Halifax, an ammunition ship in Wally's convoy sank after a fiery explosion. The rest of the convoy had to stop for repairs in Iceland. It was the second week in June 1941 before Wally finally reached England.

Wally spent most of the summer getting advanced training in Cumbria, near the Scottish border, at an Operational Training Unit (OTU) run by the Royal Air Force (RAF). He was flying Hurricane fighter planes now, battle-scarred veterans full of patched bullet holes. In the OTU, Wally learned to use his plane as a weapon. He practised formation flying, air-to-ground shooting and firing at a drogue, a long cloth tube towed by another plane. He and the other pilots staged mock "dogfights" (aerial combat) without ammunition. When they pushed the button on the steering column to fire their guns, a camera attached to the wing took pictures of what the burst would have hit. This provided a record of how accurate their "strikes" had been.

Many of Wally's instructors were veteran fighter pilots on a rest period. They tried to share their experience with the "sprogs," as they called all the new pilots who hadn't been in combat. They said you had to fly close to your target—250 yards—before you fired. Also, while both you and your foe were in motion, you had to calculate, in a split second, where to aim your guns. It was useless to fire at where the enemy fighter plane was now. Instead, you had to aim for where it would be when your burst of fire reached it. This was known as "deflection shooting." All the fighter aces could do it. The trick, they said, was to stay alive long enough to become good at it. Wally knew—as every young pilot did—that many airmen were killed in their very first combat.

The instructors also gave the sprogs some lectures on how to bail out of their planes if they were hit. Once again, it was something that had to be done very quickly, and you needed luck. One veteran flyer told Wally that the worst thing he had ever seen was a pilot plummeting helplessly to earth while his parachute burned. "It looked like a Roman candle," he said.

Not much was said about being taken prisoner, since it was far more likely that either you would make it back to your base, or you would be killed. However, it was made clear to all the air force officers that if they *were* taken prisoner by the Germans, it was their duty to try to escape.

"You have been trained at great expense," they were told, "and you ought to try to get back to your squadron and fly again."

One other remark stuck in Wally's mind. A senior British officer told them that in order to be a successful escaper, "you have to be a combination miner, actor, linguist, thief and all round tough guy." Wally chuckled to himself. I've got mining covered, he thought, and I'm in better shape than a lot of these guys. But I don't know about the other stuff.

In mid-September of 1941, Wally was posted to the RCAF's elite 401 Squadron, then based at Digby, England. They flew the most famous British fighter plane, the sleek Supermarine Spitfire. The cockpit was so small that it was said you didn't climb into a Spitfire, you put it on. Fortunately, you could adjust the pedals for the length of your legs. The bucket seat could also be moved up and down. Even so, the Plexiglas canopy didn't clear Wally's head by much. His shoulders touched each side of the cockpit.

On October 8, the Squadron received a shipment of the latest Spitfire model, the Mk VB, with a 1,440 horsepower engine, and a top speed of over 370 miles per hour. It was armed with a cannon and two machine guns on each wing. A few days later, Wally flew one of them down to the new 401 base at Biggin Hill.

Biggin Hill was an airfield known to pilots as the Bump. It stood on a windy hill in Kent, England, an hour's drive from London. When other southern England airfields were cloaked in fog, Biggin Hill was usually clear, which meant that fighter pilots could take off. The move to this airfield, so close to the coast and the English Channel, meant that Wally was going into battle.

In August and September 1940, the year before Wally came to England, 401 (then known as No. 1 Squadron) had been the only Canadian squadron to fight alongside the RAF in the Battle of Britain. In those two months, Allied fighters duelled with the Luftwaffe in the skies over England. During those desperate days, the average operational life expectancy of a fighter pilot was just 15 to 20 minutes. But the Luftwaffe had failed to destroy the RAF, and Hitler had given up his idea of invading England, at least for the present. Instead, with most of Western Europe under control, Hitler decided to shift his attention eastward. The Germans attacked Russia in June 1941.

By the time Wally joined 401, Allied Fighter Command's strategy was to sweep across the English Channel, attack the Germans occupying France and fly back home. The idea was that German squadrons who had to fight them in France would not be sent to join the fighting in Russia. Allied air force operations over France took various forms. There were large-scale fighter sweeps, intended to lure the Luftwaffe into the air and engage them. These sweeps were called "circuses" if the fighters were escorting bombers, or "rodeos" if only fighter planes were involved. When there was too much cloud cover for these large operations, there were "rhubarbs" instead. This meant that a pair of planes, flying low, would cross the channel and look for ground targets, such as troop trains or army trucks.

Despite their playful-sounding names, every kind of raid was extremely dangerous, and very costly to the air force in men and aircraft. The average operational life expectancy of a fighter pilot, although longer than during the Battle of Britain, was still only about 45 minutes. Allied sweeps cost 200 pilots in just the three months of June, July and August of 1941. By November, British

Prime Minister Winston Churchill had decided to suspend them. But that decision came too late for Wally.

On the morning of October 27, the 24 planes of 401 Squadron rendezvoused with two RAF squadrons and crossed the channel to France for a rodeo. Wally had only been on one previous raid—a rhubarb—but they had met no enemy planes and returned safely to Biggin Hill. This time, they were ambushed. German Messerschmitt fighter planes swarmed down out of the clouds where they had been waiting to intercept them.

Wally had been well trained and he was a good pilot, but without combat experience, he found it hard to make sense of the air battle. Everything was happening so fast. Wally twisted his head, looking right, left and above for enemy planes. His radio crackled with warnings from his section leader. Suddenly, a Spitfire to one side of him burst into flames and plummeted toward the earth. That shock seemed to sharpen his senses.

Wally singled out a Messerschmitt that was screaming down toward him at a sharp angle. While he was lining up the German fighter plane in his sights, another plane—one he hadn't even seen—fired a burst at him from behind. Within seconds, his plane was on fire.

There wasn't much time, and there was so much to do to get out safely. Wally knew he could not afford to panic. He slid back the Plexiglas canopy. He turned on his pipsqueak, an emergency transmitter that would allow a ground station back in England to fix his position. He could already feel the heat on his back as he unhooked his safety harness. He opened the cockpit door, struggled out onto the wing and kicked away from the plane.

As soon as he was clear, Wally pulled the ring on his chest that would inflate the parachute strapped to his back.

Was it damaged by fire?

He thought of the Roman candle he'd heard about. It was a great relief to be jerked sharply when his parachute billowed open above him.

The battle had ended as quickly as it began. The roar of engines was fading away, and he seemed to be alone in the sky. As he floated down, Wally could see the distant coast of England and safety. Unfortunately, he was coming down on the other side of the channel, and there was nothing he could do to change that.

Wally landed hard, rolling on his side as he hit the ground to spread out the impact. He had come down on a cobblestone road in the town of St. Omer, France. Automatically, he unclipped his parachute—it might drag him along the ground if he didn't. As he sat up and struggled to catch his breath, a tiny, elderly woman in a black dress hurried out of the nearest house. She was carrying a bottle of amber-coloured liquid and a glass. Without a word, she poured Wally a drink, and he downed it. It was very fine cognac. As she refilled Wally's glass, he heard shouts and looked down the road. Two German soldiers were running toward him with their guns raised.

Chapter 5

CAPTURED

The first Germans Wally Floody ever saw were the soldiers who arrested him. They had their guns pointed at him, but their faces were calm. They weren't particularly surprised to see him. Allied flyers had tumbled out of the sky near St. Omer before. They helped him to his feet and, one on either side, dragged him away from the elderly French woman with her bottle of cognac. In English, one of them said to Wally, "For you, the war is over."

Later, Wally would think about how wrong they were, but at that moment he was stunned and speechless. Just that morning he'd been having breakfast in England. He'd written a quick letter to Betty. And now he'd been in combat, seen explosions and death in the air, and fallen into the hands of the enemy. It wasn't even lunchtime yet.

Wally was held in the local police station overnight.

The next morning he was put on a train, escorted by several Luftwaffe men heading home on leave. The German policy for prisoners of war was that they were turned over to the same branch of the armed services they came from. This meant that Allied air force prisoners were the responsibility of the German air force. By and large, the Luftwaffe treated air force officers like Wally Floody humanely. There was a tradition, dating back to the First World War, that pilots on both sides of the war should respect each other as "knights of the air." In the early years of the Second World War, some of this attitude still remained.

A modern, high-speed French train took Wally and his guards as far as Brussels, Belgium. From there the ride was less luxurious—a crowded, third-class railway car on a German train to Frankfurt am Main, Germany. They arrived early in the morning, on Wally's third day of travel. People in the station stared at him curiously as his Luftwaffe guards hurried him along the platform. One woman muttered angrily under her breath as he passed by. It was an uncomfortable feeling. He was still wearing his bedraggled uniform and everyone could see that he was a prisoner of war.

The final leg of Wally's journey was made on a streetcar. On this route, people were so used to seeing prisoners that they paid him little attention. It was so odd to be seated beside ordinary people going about their daily lives: mothers taking their children to school; businessmen in suits reading their newspapers as they rode to work. They looked much the same as people in England or back in Toronto. Wally may have been sitting with them, but he didn't have an ordinary life any more. He didn't know if he would ever get it back.

Wally and his guards got off at the Oberursel stop. This was a prosperous suburb with large houses and many trees, now losing their red and gold leaves. His captors led him across a field toward a compound surrounded by a high wire fence. As they got closer he could see some RAF officers behind the wire, calling out greetings to him. For a minute Wally felt better—he wasn't alone in this.

Wally was turned over to a new set of guards, and taken into a long wooden building. It had a narrow corridor with cells on both sides. His guards stopped halfway along, shoved him into a cell and locked the door. He came to know this cell well over the next couple of days. It was only 8 feet long by 5 feet wide. There was nothing in it but a small table and a narrow bed—too short for Wally—with two thin blankets and a lumpy mattress filled with wood shavings. There was one barred window, but the glass was frosted so he couldn't see out. Sometimes it was so hot in the little room that Wally broke out in a sweat; at other times it was too cold. Later, when he had a chance to compare notes with other prisoners, they decided the Germans had changed the temperature on purpose to shake them up.

Each morning at 8:00 a.m., a guard brought black

bread and *ersatz* (substitute) coffee, a drink made from roasted acorns. At lunch there was watery soup and potatoes, and at dinner, bread and weak tea. Wally quickly learned a few essential German words: *danke* (thanks), *bitte* (please), *brot* (bread), *kaffee* (coffee) and, above all, *abort* (toilet). There was no toilet in the cell. To go to the bathroom, he had to call for a guard to escort him. If the guard shouted back, *"Abort ist besezt"* ("The toilet is occupied"), he had to wait.

There was nothing to read and no one to talk to. For the first time since he had been captured, Wally had time to think about what had happened. He felt angry and disgusted. All that training, all that effort, and he had been shot down in his first combat. He couldn't know it yet, but it had been Wally's bad luck to encounter fighter pilots from Jagdgeschwader 26 "Schlageter"—the most respected fighter unit in the Luftwaffe. It had more fighter aces than any other unit, many of them veterans of the Battle of Britain. They had shot Wally down, but at least he had not been killed. Maybe he'd be able to escape and get back in the war. He vowed to try.

On the second day, Wally was taken to a comfortable, well-furnished office and asked to fill out some forms. During his training, Wally had been told again and again: give only your name, rank and military identification number if you are captured. Wally filled out the first three lines of the form and left the rest blank. On the third day, a courteous man visited his cell, saying that he was from the International Red Cross. He might have been, but Wally thought he seemed more like a German intelligence agent. He asked too many questions about Wally's squadron and the base back in England. Wally didn't trust him. He didn't answer his questions.

On the fourth day, Wally was released into the compound he had seen when he first arrived. It turned out that this was only a transit camp, called Dulag Luft. Most prisoners stayed only a few days or weeks before being sent on. However, a few British prisoners were kept there for months to process the new prisoners. Most, like Wally, arrived with only the ragged clothes in which they were captured. They were given clothing, as well as supplies provided by the Red Cross such as toothpaste and a comb.

Meanwhile, back in Toronto, Betty had received a frightening telegram: "Regret to inform you that your husband, Pilot Officer Wallace Floody, is reported missing as a result of air operations on 27th October, 1941." This might mean he was dead, or it might not. She had no way to know for sure. Three other pilots from 401 Squadron had been reported killed on that same date. For seven agonizing days, the Floody family waited for more news.

On the evening of November 3, Betty got a surprising phone call from a stranger. He phoned to say that he had heard Wally's name mentioned in a German broadcast he had picked up on his shortwave radio.

Floody was such an unusual name that he had found her in the phone book. The broadcast had been bragging about all the pilots the Germans had captured, and it had named Wallace Floody as one of them. A few days later, the family received official confirmation from Canada's Department of National Defence. Wally was a prisoner of war.

By the time his family got the official note, Wally had been moved to a permanent camp. He travelled by train with a large group of prisoners, but it was far different from his first train ride as a prisoner. They travelled in unheated boxcars known as "forty-and-eights," so called since the First World War because they could hold 40 men or eight horses. It was a cold, uncomfortable journey. Their destination was a camp for Allied air force officers called Stalag Luft I, near the town of Barth. The camp's location, on a narrow strip of land jutting into the Baltic Sea, was bleak. There were no trees to stop the wind that blew constantly, carrying sand into the long wooden huts where the prisoners lived.

Shortly after arrival, Wally was invited to meet the camp's senior British officer, Harry "Wings" Day. (His nickname came from his rank, Wing Commander.) In his early 40s, Wings was one of the oldest prisoners, but he was a determined escaper. He had escaped through a tunnel from Dulag Luft, but had been recaptured. He had escaped from the train taking him from Dulag Luft to Barth—and been recaptured. But Wings had no

Wally in his room at Stalag Luft I, Barth. He is on the upper bunk. The other prisoners are, from the lower left, Sam Sangster of Winnipeg, an unidentified RAF man, and "Pop" Collett from New Zealand.

intention of giving up. He now wanted to form a committee at Stalag Luft I to put escape plans on a more organized footing. But before any new man could be invited to join these activities he had to be checked out very carefully. The airmen were worried that the Germans might try to plant spies in their midst. Wings questioned Wally closely about his training, about 401 Squadron, and about how he had been shot down. Fortunately, there were several other men in the camp who had known Wally back in England and could vouch for him. Then the conversation became more focused.

"And what did you do before the war, Floody?"

"Well, sir, I worked in a mine for a while."

"Did you indeed?" said Wings. "I think we might have some interesting work for you here."

Chapter 6

THE "ESCAPE-PROOF" CAMP

Many British and Commonwealth airmen had been shot down over German-occupied countries during the fighter plane and bomber raids of 1941. By early 1942, the German camps for air force prisoners were overcrowded so the Germans began building a new camp, Stalag Luft III. It would be the largest of all their camps for airmen. Stalag Luft III was near the town of Sagan, about 90 miles southeast of Berlin.

At the end of March 1942, almost all the prisoners at Stalag Luft I in Barth, including Wally Floody, were loaded into railway cars with barred windows and shipped to Sagan. Ten men sat packed into railway compartments that could comfortably seat only five or six. The train was often shunted off onto sidings to make way for other trains, and the journey took four days and four cold nights in the unheated cars.

When they finally arrived at the Sagan railway station, Wally and the other airmen were marched to the new camp. British airmen made up the largest group of prisoners, but Canadian, Australian and other Commonwealth flyers were being moved to the camp, too. There were also Polish, Czech, Dutch and Norwegian airmen who had escaped from their homelands when those countries fell to the Germans. They had been flying for the RAF when they were captured. Finally, there were a few Americans who had joined the RCAF or the RAF before their country entered the war.

As he headed for the new camp, Wally did not look much like the young pilot who had been shot down over France. He had now been a "kriegie" (short for *kriegsgefangener*, the German word for war prisoner) for six months. Like all the other officers, he tried to keep clean, but his clothes were shabby. Wally had parts of his own uniform, much mended, plus a sweater and woollen hat sent by the Red Cross. He had grown a scraggly beard, and he had lost a lot of weight on prison rations. He now weighed perhaps 170 pounds—much too thin for a man who was 6 feet 4 inches tall. Still, Wally remained cheerful and friendly. He was always working on an escape plan, and that kept him from getting depressed.

At Barth, Wally had become part of a group of kriegies who were dedicated to escaping. They included Wings Day and Peter Fanshawe, a Royal Navy pilot. They had started tunnels in that camp, but the site was so close to the sea that they always flooded. Now, as Wally, Wings and Peter walked through the gates of the new camp together, they were aware that the Germans considered it escape-proof. Well, they would see about that.

It was clear that the Germans were serious about keeping their troublesome prisoners penned up. Two barbed-wire fences, about 7 feet apart, surrounded the new camp. Each fence was about 9 feet high and the tops were bent inward toward the camp. Scaling those fences would be very difficult. In addition, the space between the fences was filled with tangles of barbed wire.

About 30 feet inside the fence, a piece of wire ran all around the camp, about 2 feet off the ground. This was the warning wire; the Germans warned that anyone stepping over it would be shot. There were guard towers about every 100 yards along the fence. When Wally looked up, he could see that the guards were already in place, holding semi-automatics and machine guns, and scowling down at the prisoners. The towers also had powerful searchlights mounted on them. At night these would rake the camp, picking out anyone trying to escape.

For a minute, Wally felt a surge of anger and frustration that was hard to control. Some men had been known to go "wire happy," trying suicidal rushes over the fence or out the gate. But Wally had no intention of going over that fence. His specialty was going under— and he was sure that, in the end, this was his best chance of getting home. This new location was much dryer than the one at Barth. But there were other challenges.

As Wally and Peter approached the barracks that would be their new home, some of them became obvious.

"Have a look at this," Peter said to Wally in a low voice. "They've built the huts right up off the ground."

In Barth they had tunnelled down through the floors of their huts, but if they tried that here, the guards would discover it right away.

"Yes, but see where the chimneys are?" Wally said. "It looks like they go right down into the ground. Maybe that's the way to do it."

The two men could see more problems as they looked around the camp. All the huts were at least 40 yards from the fence. In addition, the Germans had cut down all the trees on the ground beyond the camp. It appeared to be at least 100 feet from the fence to the dark pine woods where a tunnel could come up safely. Nevertheless, Wally was determined to start digging as soon as possible. But first he had to become better acquainted with his new camp and the people who ran it.

The officers' area of Stalag Luft III, where Wally was held, was known as the East Compound. A separate compound held non-commissioned officers such as flight sergeants. The camp also had a *Kommandantur*, an area with housing and offices for the Germans. Finally, there was the *Vorlager*, which contained sick quarters, a bathhouse, a coal shed, and storage buildings. The Vorlager also held the "cooler." The cooler was a small prison block where unruly kriegies were placed for a few days of solitary confinement.

Wally and other prisoners at Stalag Luft III. Clockwise from top left: Sam Sangster, John Weir, Henry (Hank) Birkland and Wally Floody.

The long wooden huts in the East Compound were newer and cleaner than the one Wally had left behind, but otherwise very similar. Each hut had 12 large rooms with six double-tiered bunks in each, and two rooms with two double-tiered bunks. Each room also had a small stove to provide heat. All the rooms had large windows to let in light and air, but the Germans locked and shuttered them at night.

The men could shave and take cold baths or showers in wash huts fitted with cold water taps and metal sinks. They could have hot showers only when groups of them were marched to the Vorlager under guard. The kriegies set aside unoccupied rooms for a library and recreation areas, and turned one empty barracks into a theatre. There was even a small sports field where the prisoners could get some exercise.

It wasn't luxurious, but Stalag Luft III was one of the better-run POW (prisoner-of-war) camps in Germany. The Kommandant, Colonel Friedrich-Wilhelm von Lindeiner, had won the Iron Cross for bravery in the First World War. He was well educated and fluent in English. He advised the prisoners that they should give up any attempts to escape from this new camp. The senior Allied officers who dealt with von Lindeiner, including Wings Day, considered him an honourable man. Still, they intended to ignore his advice.

Most of the prisoners, including Wally, saw very little of von Lindeiner. The German guards they saw every day fell into two categories, named by the prisoners "goons" and "ferrets." Many of the goons (whose name came from some large, stupid characters in a popular comic strip) were too old for military service, or considered medically unfit for it. The prisoners felt confident they could outwit them. The ferrets, on the other hand, were guards who took their work very seriously. They were alert to any hint of escape plans and specialized in uncovering tunnels under construction.

Wally soon learned to be wary of the man in charge of the ferrets, a sergeant named Herman Glemnitz. The prisoners couldn't resist playing on his name to refer to him as "Dimwitz." However, they all knew he was anything but dim.

From the beginning, the kriegies kept Glemnitz and the other guards on their toes. During the first months at Stalag Luft III, many prisoners began digging tunnels. They met problems right away.

The surface soil of the camp was grey dirt, but underneath was heavy yellow sand, treacherous and shifting. Most tunnels were very amateurish efforts that caved in within days or weeks. The guards didn't even have to search for them; they would simply drive heavy trucks around the camp. That was all it took to collapse the simple tunnels that were only a few feet down. Working separately, Peter and Wally began tunnels that were well below ground. But even these were discovered.

Meanwhile, other kinds of escapes were also going on at Stalag Luft III. One pair of kriegies arranged for their friends to create a disturbance that drew the attention of the guards in the towers. They then stepped over the warning wire, cut through the fences and barbed wire and ran into the woods. Others sneaked out among work parties of Russian prisoners, or hid in trucks that came to the camp to bring food and other supplies.

Wings Day tried to walk out the front gate, carrying a

cardboard briefcase and disguised as a German accountant (accountants visited the camp regularly to do paperwork), but a guard recognized him. He was thrown into the cooler. He and another kriegie then cut through the bars of their cell window with a small hacksaw blade that Wings had long carried, hidden in his shoe. After dark one night, as they were squeezing through the window, they were discovered by a guard. Wings drew another two-week stint in the cooler for that stunt.

While all these efforts showed courage and ingenuity, few prisoners even made it past the fence. No one managed to remain free for more than a couple of days before being recaptured. Wally remained convinced that tunnelling was his best hope.

Prisoners continued to arrive at Stalag Luft III. One of them was a wounded American named George Harsh who had been a bomber-gunner in the RCAF. Wally was writing a letter home when George arrived. Prisoners were allowed to send only three letters a month, and George had not yet been given permission to write. "I'm writing my wife, Betty, in Toronto," Wally told him. "If there's anyone in the States you want to inform that you're a prisoner and not dead, I'll get her to contact them."

George appreciated Wally's generosity, since the official letter forms were small and every word in a letter home was precious. The two men became friends. Eventually George trusted Wally with a story that no one else in the camp knew. As a teenager in Georgia, he had killed a store clerk during an armed robbery. He had been sent to prison and had been on a chain gang for six years until he received a pardon. George deeply regretted what he had done. When he joined the air force, he had hoped that by fighting against Hitler, he could make amends for his past.

Soon there were many more Americans in the camp. The United States had entered the war in December 1941, and by the middle of 1942, downed American airmen were being brought in as prisoners. The huts in the East Compound became overcrowded, with double bunks turned into triples. The Germans decided to build a new, larger compound for the prisoners, to be known as the North Compound. The kriegies with escape on their minds felt sure this would open up new opportunities. And now there was a man in the camp to get their efforts organized as never before. He was RAF Squadron Leader Roger Bushell.

The Gestapo—the ruthless Nazi secret police—brought Roger Bushell to Stalag Luft III in the fall of 1942. Wally had never met him before, but Wings Day had known him back at Dulag Luft. Roger had escaped twice, and the second time had managed to elude capture for months. A family in Prague, Czechoslovakia, hid him while he tried to arrange safe passage to Yugoslavia or Turkey. However, when his hiding place was discovered by the Gestapo, they executed the whole family. This had given Roger a deep hatred for the Nazis. He was determined to wage war in the only way left to him: by planning an escape for 200 men. It would be the biggest, most disruptive breakout ever from a German POW camp.

To put his plan into effect, he assembled a group of experienced escapers that would be known as the X Organization. Roger, overseeing the plan, would be Big X. And he wanted Wally to be a key member of his team.

Chapter 7

THE X ORGANIZATION

Early in 1943, Roger called a meeting of half a dozen or so key members of the X Organization, including Peter Fanshawe and Wally. Wings Day was not present; soon after Roger's arrival, he had been sent to another camp.

"In a few weeks, we'll all be moving into the new compound," Roger said. "This is a golden opportunity and we're going to make the most of it."

The men nodded their heads. Over the last couple of months, some of the prisoners had volunteered to help in the building of the North Compound. In particular, they had asked if they could build a theatre. The Germans had agreed. While "helping out," the work parties of prisoners had noted every detail of construction and German security measures. They had secretly measured distances from the various huts to the fences. They had estimated, as closely as they could, the distance from the fence to the pine woods beyond the camp. As soon as they moved to the new compound, they'd be ready to go into action.

"This time we'll dig three tunnels, all underway at the same time." Roger continued. "If the goons find one, they'll think that's it. And we'll keep going with the other ones."

"That's a lot of sand to get rid of, Roger," said Peter Fanshawe. His role in the X Organization was sand dispersal. "For every three feet of tunnel, we can figure one to one-and-a-half tons of sand. We can put some under the huts, but the ferrets are checking all the time to see if the level of dirt goes up. And that bright yellow colour—you can see it a mile away."

"Well, you've got a couple of weeks to come up with a solution," Roger replied. Peter lapsed into thought.

Wally, who had agreed to be the "Tunnel King," the man in charge of tunnelling operations, reported next. "We know that von Lindeiner has sensitive microphones planted nine feet below the ground, all over the compound. We know what they're there for—to pick up any vibrations from tunnel digging. So," Wally concluded, "it's pretty obvious. We'll go where they can't hear us—thirty feet straight down. Then we'll start the tunnels from there.

"The sand is treacherous," Wally continued. "You can never pack it hard enough that it won't come down on you. We'll have to shore up the whole thing—walls and roof. It'll be hard to find that much wood."

By the end of the meeting, every man had an assignment. One man, for instance, would be in charge of getting wood for the tunnels; another would be in charge of befriending and bribing the guards; yet another would look after forging the documents the escapers would need once they were free.

Roger closed the meeting by saying, "We'll need tighter security than we've ever had before. I don't ever want to hear the word "tunnel" again. We'll call them Tom, Dick and Harry. And I want a watch placed on every guard. No goon or ferret is going to take a step in the camp that we don't know about, day or night."

"I know just the man to organize that," said Wally. "I'll get George Harsh."

At the beginning of April, the officers in the East Compound moved into the North Compound. More prisoners were brought in from other camps, including Wings Day. His friends in the X Organization were happy to see him again. He had made several unsuccessful escape attempts at his most recent camp, but was still game to be part of the X Organization's plan.

Soon there were about 1,500 men in the North Compound. Air force officer prisoners were not made to work by the Germans, and they had a great deal of empty time to fill. At least 600 of them would busy themselves by working on the escape in some way.

The North Compound had 15 huts, arranged in three rows. Just as in the old compound, the huts were raised, but the brick and concrete bases under the stoves went right down into the ground. In addition, the huts in the North Compound had their own kitchens and washrooms with concrete floors and drains that also went into the ground. Stoves, kitchens, washrooms: these were the only places the tunnels could start.

Wally and the tunnelling team quickly decided on three tunnel sites. The shortest distance to the trees was on the west side of the compound. So Tom and Dick would go west, Tom from hut 123 and Dick from hut 122. But Harry would take a longer route northward from hut 104. It would have to go under the Vorlager before it reached the woods. Harry would be about 350 feet long—longer than any tunnel Wally had dug before. But he knew the Germans wouldn't be expecting a tunnel on that side of the camp.

The trapdoors that would form the entrance to the tunnels were designed by a group of Polish airmen. Tom's trap went through a concrete floor in a dimly lit passageway beside the kitchen of hut 123. The Poles cast a square of concrete, using cement stolen while the camp was being built. It exactly matched the hole they cut in the floor. Dick's trapdoor was also made of concrete, but it was under a sunken drain, about 18 inches square, in the washroom floor of hut 122. Since there were always a few inches of washwater sitting in the drain, it was perfectly disguised.

The layout of the North Compound, Stalag Luft III,
showing the routes of the three tunnels.

Harry's trap was under a stove in hut 104. The stove sat on a square base made of small ceramic tiles. The Poles lifted each tile separately and glued them into a wooden tray, which became the trapdoor for Harry. The kriegies made an extension for the stove's chimney pipe with empty powdered milk cans, so they could use the stove even when it was off its base. A passing guard would see normal smoke wafting from the chimney.

Putting in the traps was risky. It had to be done in full view, not underground, and breaking through brick and concrete was noisy work. Kriegies were stationed outside the huts, banging away at innocent metal projects to disguise the noise. The prisoners were constantly making pots and pans out of milk cans, so the guards thought nothing of it. Other prisoners staged boisterous sports matches, and even loud choir practices. But safest of all was knowing that the guards were nowhere near while you were working.

George Harsh's security team was up to the challenge. At first George had wanted nothing to do with the escape. But he felt he owed Wally a favour, and he was touched that Wally had faith in him. George turned out to be the ideal man for the job. There had always been a system of "stooges" in the camp—men who kept watch on the activities of German guards. But George made the system more thorough. His 200 stooges kept track of every single goon or ferret who came into the compound. He kept their shifts short so that they would stay alert.

*The stove, standing on a tiled base,
hid the trapdoor for Harry.*

The stooges used an elaborate system of signals to pass along warnings to people doing X Organization work. For example, a stooge stationed near the gates of the compound might see Herman Glemnitz headed in the direction of hut 122, where work was underway. He would place a Red Cross box on top of a garbage can. Another stooge watching from a window in hut 122 would see this signal and give the alarm. "Ferrets! Pack up!" By the time Glemnitz got to hut 122, the tunnel trap would be closed and invisible. All he would find were a few prisoners shaving or washing their hands.

As soon as the traps were in, Wally and the other tunnellers started digging the 30-foot shafts. It was cramped work in the shafts, and the deeper they went, the darker it got. Wally worked by the flickering light of a margarine lamp. It kept going out, and he realized that was because there wasn't enough oxygen to feed it. But he kept working, lungs wheezing and head pounding. He told himself this was the toughest stage.

The tunnellers framed the shafts with wood and shored them by jamming flat boards in the spaces between the frames. Then they began to carve out three workrooms at the base of each tunnel. One would be for sand storage and bagging. The second would be a workroom in which to cut the board lengths for shoring. The third room was the most important of all. It was for the air pump.

A Norwegian airman named Jens Muller had designed the pump. It was made from two canvas kit bags,

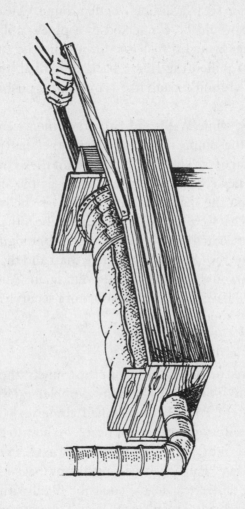

The tunnel air pump was made from two kit bags sewn together.

sewn together and reinforced with hoops of wire. The bag was then set in a sliding wooden frame. One end of the pump would be connected to a pipe—milk cans again—that brought fresh air down from the surface. When you pulled the frame back and forth, the bag would deflate and expand like a concertina, pushing air into the tunnel.

One day, while Wally and two other men were digging out the pump room for Harry, the shaft above them began to trickle sand. In an instant they saw their danger. They scrambled up the ladder as the shoring cracked and the shaft caved in. Wally was the last up, and his legs were trapped in sand. The other two hauled him out. It was a close call, and he figured it wouldn't be the last one. The whole shaft and the three chambers would have to be dug out again. And this time they'd have to shore them up more securely.

There were two basic facts about the tunnels: they disgorged sand—tons of it—and they gobbled up wood.

Fortunately, Peter Fanshawe had come up with an ingenious solution for the first problem: how to get rid of the sand right under the guards' noses. He invented "trouser bags." Pairs of these long narrow bags—made from long underwear legs—could be filled with sand and hidden inside a man's pant legs. The bottom ends of the bags were held shut with clothes pegs attached to strings. The other ends of the strings were in the man's pockets.

The men who carried the sand were soon nicknamed "penguins," for their slightly waddling walk. When the penguins arrived at a safe place to spread the sand, they pulled the strings in their pockets. Two thin streams of sand would pour out on their shoes, to be trodden quickly into the ground. One favourite spot for penguin sand drops was the "circuit" around the camp where the prisoners liked to walk each day. Another good place was the vegetable gardens some prisoners had started with seeds sent by the Red Cross. Here the ground was turned up anyway, so snooping ferrets would expect to see some yellow sand.

The second problem was the wood supply. Even before they began digging, the tunnellers knew where to get it. Their basic shoring materials would be the flat bed boards from the kriegies' bunks. These bed boards were 2 feet wide. That dictated the width and height of the shafts and tunnels—a 2-foot square. This provided just enough space for a man to squeeze through. The real difficulty was that these bed boards were in limited supply. They could hardly ask the Germans to replace the ones they took. So, at first, the tunnellers tried to get by with as little shoring as possible. But whenever Wally tried to go ahead a few feet without it, he paid the price. There were small falls of sand in the tunnels almost every day, and one that buried Wally and almost killed him.

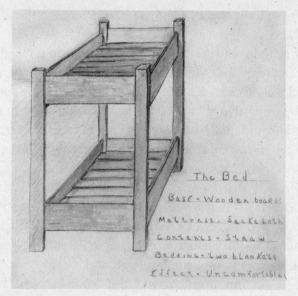

The Bed
Base - Wooden boards
Mattress - Sackcloth
Contents - Straw
Bedding - Two blankets
Effect - Uncomfortable

Wally's drawing of his Stalag Luft III bunk, in his journal. It shows all the bed boards, the main source of shoring for the tunnel.

At first the X Organization asked for just one or two boards from each kriegie's bed, but eventually they took even more. The tunnels used 4,000 bed boards.

Here is a list of just *some* of the other materials used to construct Tom, Dick and Harry. A much longer list of what was missing from the camp was later compiled by the Germans.

34 chairs
52 20-man tables
10 single tables
76 benches
90 double-tiered bunks
1,219 knives
478 spoons
582 forks
69 lamps
246 water cans
30 shovels
1,000 feet of electric wire
600 feet of rope
3,424 towels (many of these were used by
the penguins)

In the end, every one of the 1,500 men in the North Compound made at least this contribution to the escape: they slept on sagging, uncomfortable bunks.

Chapter 8

TOM, DICK AND HARRY

Wally often thought of what he'd once been told about escaping: "You have to be a combination miner, actor, linguist, thief and all round tough guy." People who fit all of these descriptions were in Stalag Luft III and working for the X Organization. In fact, many other talents could have been added to the list, including forger, mapmaker and tailor.

Tunnelling out of the camp had little point if the men were immediately recognizable for what they were: escaped prisoners of war. To have any hope of success, they had to blend in. From the escaper's point of view, the good thing about wartime Germany was that so many people were on the move from one place to another, including soldiers on leave or going to a new posting, and civilians leaving bombed-out city homes to stay with relatives in the countryside. There were also many non-Germans working in the country in various war-related industries—good possibilities for fake identities. However, for escapers, the bad thing about wartime Germany was that it was a tightly regulated country. Every person had to carry an identity card. Soldiers had to carry a paybook and other papers. Foreign workers had to have documents permitting them to travel. The escapers would need to carry these documents, too. Men with artistic and drafting talents were put to work providing them. They had no typewriters. Instead, they used India ink and a fine nib pen or a fine paintbrush to forge "typed" and "printed" papers that were very convincing. They even carved boot heels to make "official" stamps for these documents.

Other men were busy making maps and compasses. Each escaper would need maps. There wasn't enough time to draw and hand-colour all of them. Instead, the mapmakers mixed up the jelly powder sent to them in Red Cross parcels and let the jelly set in big flat pans. They laid an original map on the jelly while the map's ink was still wet. Then they laid thin sheets of paper on the jelly to pick up an impression. Usually they could make about 20 copies before the ink ran out. Using this method, they made more than 1,000 maps.

Meanwhile, other men patiently stroked razor blades with a horseshoe magnet, always moving in the same direction. It took hours, but in the end the blades would become magnetized. Then they were cut into slivers to become compass needles. The compass cases were moulded from melted-down phonograph records.

The escapers also needed convincing clothes. Men in the camp who had tailoring experience went to work. Their basic materials were air force uniforms and blankets. These could be dyed and cut into all kinds of outfits. For dyes, they used ink, boot polish, beet juice, or dye made by boiling cloth bookcovers. They made clothes for businessmen and workmen, and even military uniforms. A blue-grey RAF uniform could be turned into a grey Luftwaffe uniform by rubbing ash into the fabric. Silver buttons and insignia were cast in moulds carved out of bars of soap, using melted silver paper.

Not everything could be made. For instance, cameras had to be smuggled into the camp, to take photos for identity cards. The source for such things was often a German guard. Some X Organization men who were fluent German speakers specialized in the slow but ruthless process of "taming a goon." It often started with a casual chat about the weather to a guard who was bored and lonely. After several weeks of idle conversation, the guard might be invited to have a cup of coffee in the kriegie's room. The prisoners received coffee in food parcels sent by the International Red Cross. Most Germans hadn't had real coffee since before the war, so it was very tempting. The guard would be offered a bar of chocolate—also from the Red Cross parcel—to take home to his wife and children on his next leave. Again, this was a treat he couldn't get elsewhere. Eventually, the guard would be asked to bring in something in return—like a hammer or pliers or a camera. The guard would likely refuse at first. Then the kriegie would gently hint that the Kommandant might be interested to hear about the food the guard had accepted. The guard was trapped, and had to continue smuggling, becoming what was known as "a tame goon."

Once the shafts for Tom, Dick and Harry were finished, the tunnellers settled into two shifts a day. The diggers worked in two-man teams, with the first shift starting right after breakfast and the second finishing about dinnertime. Wally often paired up with another Canadian named Hank Birkland. They had a lot in common. Hank had also ridden the rails before the war, and had worked in a gold mine in British Columbia.

Wally and Hank had to work lying on their sides or stomachs. They couldn't sit up and they couldn't turn around in their cramped space. One would hack at the tunnel face while the other bagged up the loose sand. Wally soon noticed that when Hank was digging, he tended to veer to the right. So he made sure that John Weir would dig the next shift, because he tended to veer to the left.

Digging was such hot, sweaty work that some of the tunnellers preferred to work naked. But they ended up with scrapes—the kriegies called them "sand burns"—all over their bodies. Wally was afraid that the guards would spot the scrapes and become suspicious. For that reason, he decreed that the diggers had to wear long underwear. These longjohns were filthy and soaked with perspiration by the end of a shift. The diggers were happy to peel them off and stow them at the bottom of the shaft.

As the tunnels stretched farther and farther from the shaft, it became too exhausting to haul each bag of sand back to the rooms at the foot of the shaft. Wally, thinking back to his mining days, suggested some kind of track and cart system. Soon inventive kriegies had designed and built one for each tunnel. The tracks were made from long strips of wood used to reinforce the walls and ceilings of the huts. Wooden crates were turned into wagons. The wheels were made from three discs of wood glued together. The disc in the middle was smaller, forming a groove that fitted into the rail. The wagons could carry 200 pounds of sand back to the shaft. Men could also use them to roll to and from the digging face. And there was another improvement: the inventors rigged up pipelines, made from the ever-useful milk cans joined together, to carry fresh air from the pump to the digging faces.

All three tunnels were now moving forward by 3 to 4 feet each day. It was going far better than Wally had dared to hope.

* * *

"We've got trouble," George Harsh announced one afternoon early in June, when Wally came up from a digging shift. After Wally had cleaned himself up, he went outside to see what George was talking about. On the south side of the camp, an army of workmen had moved in. They were taking down the trees and digging up the ground. The kriegies soon found out why: the Germans were building yet another compound at Stalag Luft III. By the autumn, they were going to move all the Americans out and put them in their own separate compound. George Harsh would be all right—the Germans considered him an RCAF officer. But many other American airmen had worked hard on tunnelling, security and other jobs. It looked as if they would lose their chance to go out in the tunnels.

It might just be possible to finish a tunnel before the Germans moved the Americans. The X committee held a quick meeting and decided to throw all their efforts into Tom. It was already 60 feet long. It had the shortest route under the wire and to the trees. Wally thought that if shifts worked around the clock, they could dig perhaps 10 feet a day. They had more than 200 feet to go.

"Every cloud has a silver lining. If we have to shut down Dick, we can use it to hide the sand from Tom, " Peter Fanshawe said cheerfully. Wally groaned at the thought of putting sand into the place he had spent so much effort digging out. But he had to admit it made sense. Dick was in hut 122, right next door to Tom.

The tunnellers made an exhausting, all-out effort to finish Tom in time to get the Americans out with the other escapers. By the end of August 1943, Tom was under the wire and getting close to the trees. Then they had yet another setback. The Germans brought in another crew to cut down trees. This time they were working on the west side of the camp, where Tom would come up. Wally had thought they might be two days away from the trees. Now it looked more like 10.

It was clear that the Germans were convinced a tunnel was underway. They focused on hut 123, an obvious site because it was close to the fence. One day they dug a trench between hut 123 and the fence, hoping to hit a tunnel.

Roger Bushell and Wally watched from a discreet distance. Roger was concerned, but Wally was not. "We're 30 feet down, remember. I predict the ferrets will give up long before that." It was a hot day. The Germans gave up after 5 feet.

The ferrets under the command of Herman Glemnitz stepped up their sudden, nerve-wracking searches. They struck in the daytime and at night. On one occasion, the men guarding the top of the tunnel had only 20 seconds' warning to get the trap closed and disguise the entrance. But they did it.

Wally and the other tunnellers kept digging. By the beginning of September, Tom was 260 feet long, and

Wally calculated they should be in the trees. Now they just had to wait for the next moonless night to escape.

The ferrets kept up the pressure on hut 123. They poked the ground around it with long, thin metal probes. They got down on their hands and knees and scanned the floor. On September 8, just when they were about to give up for the day, a ferret dropped his metal probe. It hit Tom's concrete trapdoor and chipped off a corner. Purely by accident, Tom had been discovered. The Germans were triumphant. They blew the tunnel up.

The only way Wally could cope with the sickening disappointment was to get back to work. He and his tunnellers returned to Harry. He had been under the wire and into the trees with Tom. Now, once again, he had hundreds of feet to go.

The Americans moved to the South Compound a few days later, losing their last chance at the X Organization's tunnels. Meanwhile the Germans kept clearing the trees on the west side of the camp, to build yet another compound. Now there was no chance that Dick, the tunnel from hut 122, would ever be reopened. There was only one tunnel left, one chance to escape.

Roger decided that it was too dangerous to continue. They would have to wait a few months and hope that the ferrets would relax their guard. Roger ordered Wally to shut down Harry.

Chapter 9

ONE DAY AT A TIME

With the tunnel shut down for a few months, Wally lost the work that was most important to him. But he was determined to stay positive. As George Harsh told Wally, prison life had to be taken one day at a time.

The day began with *appell*, the roll call. Wally and the other prisoners had to line up in rows on the sports field while the guards counted them to make sure no one had escaped. There would be at least one appell later in the day, and sometimes several more. After morning appell, many kriegies walked "the circuit" around the perimeter of the camp to chat and get some exercise. Their favourite topic of discussion was how the war was going.

Although the men were prisoners, they were not cut off from the news. The Germans broadcast their news over loudspeakers in the camp, and the men could get a translation from prisoners who spoke German. But the kriegies were also getting the BBC news from England, on their own hidden radios. These radios were designed and built in the camp, using such items as empty cookie tins for the variable condensers, as well as parts brought in by the "tame goons." The stooge system protected these radios as carefully as the tunnels. Very few kriegies heard the actual broadcasts, but they were passed on quietly to small groups of men throughout the day.

After the circuit, the men drifted off. Each one, in his own way, had to face the challenge of filling his day.

Wally was reminded every time he looked at the high wire fence that his freedom had been taken away. He could not go home, he could not see friends and family, he could not even be alone with his thoughts. There was no privacy anywhere, not even in the bathroom.

Wally lived in a room that was about 16 feet square, shared by eight men sleeping in double bunks. The room also had a table, a stove for heat and making tea or coffee, and three lockers for the kriegies' clothes and other belongings. Wally and the other men put their lockers in the hall to make a little more space in the room.

At one end of their hut was a room with a row of toilets, and in the middle of the hut, there was a washroom and a kitchen. The washroom had only sinks, but the prisoners rigged up their own shower heads. However, they had to take their showers in cold water. As in the

East Compound, they could get hot showers in the Vor-lager, but only when the Germans marched them there.

Once a week, Wally did his laundry in the washroom. He used a metal bucket and soap shavings cut from a bar of soap. To wash his clothes he used a handy invention the kriegies called "the prison Maytag." It was a stick with two cans attached to the end, one inside the other. The larger can had holes punched in the sides. When he plunged the stick up and down in the bucket

The kriegies share a cookstove. The original watercolour was painted directly into Wally's journal. The artist is unknown.

of clothes, the small can would move inside the other and force water out the holes. Wally churned the laundry for about half an hour, then rinsed the clothes and hung them up on the line.

The kitchen had a coal stove on which the kriegies could cook their dinner. The men in each room would take turns making the meals for their roommates. Since food for about 100 men had to be prepared on one stove, they drew up a schedule so that everyone got a chance at the burners.

Food was the obsession of every man in Stalag Luft III, because there was never quite enough. Germany had signed the Geneva Convention in 1929. This document outlined the humane treatment that prisoners of war must receive. Allied prisoners of war were fed regularly, except for Russians, whose government had not signed the Geneva Convention, and who were harshly mistreated by the Germans. However, the food was unappetizing—mostly root vegetables and small pieces of low-quality meat—and the portions were stingy. They were also given "cheese" made from fish waste, which had a revolting smell, and "coffee" made from acorns.

The basic kriegie food was hard, dry black bread, served at breakfast, lunch and dinner. The men knew it was hard to digest and not very nutritious. But it wasn't until after the war, when the recipe turned up in captured German files, that they found out what was in it. In addition to rye grain and sliced sugar beets, the bread sometimes contained "tree flour"—another term for sawdust—as well as minced leaves and straw. To help them choke down the bread, the kriegies had jam with little or no fruit in it, and margarine. All in all, their diet provided about 1,600 calories per day, about 1,000 less than the average man needs. Tunnel diggers, of course, needed even more.

Fortunately, under the Geneva Convention, prisoners of war were also allowed to receive food parcels from the International Red Cross. The contents were slightly different depending on which country sent them. Canadian parcels featured real butter, for instance; British parcels had treasured extras like mustard and pepper packets; the American parcels contained real coffee. All of them had canned meat, such as SPAM (processed ham) and corned beef, cookies, chocolate, cheese, dried fruit and canned powdered milk, called KLIM. If each man had received one parcel a week as intended, the prisoners would have been well fed. But in the chaos of war, the parcels didn't arrive regularly, so the kriegies were always malnourished. Most men slowly lost weight and strength.

Even the Red Cross parcels provided only a few different kinds of food. The prisoners ate the same meals, day after day. The only tiny variation came at dinnertime. One day they might have fried corned beef and the next day, fried SPAM.

The kriegies tried their best—some with more success than others—to turn their limited ingredients into something more interesting. Wally was notorious for a dessert he concocted. He called it "trifle," but his friends called it "Floody's Folly." It started with a layer of "chocolate glop" (melted chocolate mixed with powdered milk), then a dried fruit layer, a peanut butter and prune layer, a coffee fudge (melted chocolate mixed with coffee) layer and a topping of "whipped cream" (powdered milk whipped with margarine). He thought enough of his recipe to write it in his prisoner-of-war log. This was a sturdy journal that the YMCA had sent to all prisoners of war.

Pages and pages of Wally's journal were devoted to food. The always-hungry kriegies traded elaborate recipes for pheasant and other mouth-watering dishes that they could make after the war. Wally copied them into his journal, as well as addresses and remembered menus from prisoners' favourite restaurants.

Wally wrote to his wife, his parents and his sister as often as he was allowed to—three letters and four postcards a month. Like all the prisoners, he looked forward to receiving letters from home, but they also made him aware of how much he was missing. One letter from his mother told him that his grandfather had died. His younger sister, Catherine, wrote to tell Wally that she would soon be graduating as a nurse. And then another letter came saying that she had met a doctor and they planned to get married. Betty wrote that she had a job in Toronto now, and had also become the vice president of the Canadian Prisoner of War Relatives' Association. She answered questions for concerned families who were wondering what they were allowed to send their imprisoned sons and husbands. She also gave many speeches about prisoners of war and made sure the newspapers didn't forget about the men imprisoned overseas.

From time to time, Wally would receive official word that his rank had automatically been raised, first to Flying Officer, and by the end of the war, to Flight Lieutenant. He found this grimly amusing. More fun was a letter he got from the company that had made his silk parachute, welcoming him to the Caterpillar Club of airmen whose lives had been saved by bailing out. Eventually they sent Wally a small gold pin of a caterpillar (a silk spinner), which he wore for the rest of his life. He pasted the letter in his journal.

Some prisoners filled their days by playing in the camp orchestra or working in the camp theatre as actors, directors, scene painters or stagehands. Wally had always been too busy digging tunnels to get involved with any of these activities. However, after Harry was shut down, Wally did take some classes. There were some very well educated prisoners at Stalag Luft III and many of them gave classes. Prisoners could study a foreign language, science, economics, mathematics, English literature and dozens of other subjects. After the war, Wally often said that Stalag Luft III was almost like a university for him.

Wally, like the other kriegies, did a lot of "tin bashing." The Germans gave the prisoners very few cooking utensils, so they made their own pots and pans by cutting and soldering metal from their powdered milk cans. Wally also built some extra chairs for his room, using wood from the crates in which the Red Cross food parcels had been shipped. Wally enjoyed the challenge of designing and making useful things. It passed the time, and when he was finished, he had something that made his life OK.

Toward the end of 1943, two events lifted Wally's spirits. As soon as the weather was cold enough in December, the Canadian kriegies flooded a portion of a sports field for a hockey rink. Back in Stalag Luft I at Barth, the prisoners had taken metal brackets off benches and attached them to their shoes for skate blades. But Conn Smythe, the owner of the Toronto Maple Leafs, and some other hockey enthusiasts had arranged for Stalag Luft III to receive real hockey equipment. They had enough skates and sticks for two teams: the North American Officers and the Officers of the Rest of the World. Hockey had never been Wally's game back in Canada, but now he was happy to do his bit to help win the championship for the North American (almost entirely Canadian) team.

The second treat was a special Christmas dinner

Menu for Christmas dinner, 1943,
pasted into Wally's journal.

parcel sent by the Red Cross. Wally and the other kriegies dined on salmon with sauce, sausages and bacon,
pork and vegetables, and for dessert, Christmas pud-
ding with real, canned, cream. They toasted each other
with a homebrew they had made from fermented
raisins. Wally had now spent three Christmases behind
barbed wire. He hoped this would be the last.

Chapter 10

STARTING AGAIN

On January 10, 1944, Roger gave the order to re-open Harry. He believed that the Germans would not expect tunnelling in the dead of winter. But if the diggers put in a good two months' work on the tunnel, they could be ready for a breakout in early spring.

The trap had been so well sealed that it took two hours to pry it open. When Wally got down into the tunnel, he was pleased to see that it was still in good shape. Only four of the bed boards had warped, creating a few minor sand leaks, but no cave ins. The canvas kit bags used for the air pump had rotted and would have to be replaced. The repairs were made quickly. Within four days, Wally and Hank and the other tunnelling crews were able to return to their shifts.

Soon Harry was wired for electric lighting, thanks to a large roll of wire that a careless electrician had left unguarded in the camp. The kreigies secretly tapped into the camp's electrical supply. During the daytime hours, the Germans kept the electricity turned off. The tunnellers had to stick to their smelly, smoky margarine lamps. But once the camp's electricity came on, they could work long into the evening in a blaze of light.

By late January, Harry had passed the 100-foot mark. The tunnel faced a wood shortage. Some kriegies now had no bed boards at all. Their mattresses rested on webs of rope attached to their bed frames. Fortunately, some of the huts had double floors and some had double walls, so the X Organization took the wood from the inner layer. "You know," George Harsh said one day, "a strong wind would probably blow the whole camp down."

The diggers enlarged the tunnel for a halfway house that they called Piccadilly Circus, after a busy intersection in London. One set of tracks ended here and another began. There was room in Piccadilly Circus for two men to turn around. So the digging pairs no longer had to go all the way back to the shaft to exchange positions. During the escape, men could be stationed here to help the escapers through the tunnel. The tunnellers were now under the Vorlager, with the Germans overhead. They had to work as quietly as possible.

Winter weather gave the X Organization an unforeseen problem. They couldn't disperse sand outside if it had snowed. Once again Peter Fanshawe's team came up with a solution. They would stow the sand under the floor of the theatre. Penguins carried the sand from the tunnel to the theatre in 35-pound bags, hidden under winter overcoats.

By mid-February, Harry was past the 200-foot mark. A second halfway house, named Leicester Square, was built. The cooler was directly above Leicester Square, and sometimes the tunnellers could hear the faint tapping of the guards' boots on the concrete floor.

Wally began to let himself hope that this time the tunnel was really going to succeed.

"I'm in training," he wrote to Betty, "for the same kind of work I did before the war." When she read that, Betty almost dropped the letter. "Wally's digging a tunnel!" she said to herself.

Soon it was time for the X Organization to choose the 200 men who would escape through the tunnel. They had a list of more than 500 names—all men who had worked on the escape plan and were interested in going out. Some men who had worked hard on the escape were claustrophobic—afraid of enclosed spaces—and took themselves off the list. One of these was an Australian named Paul Brickhill, who would later make the story of the escape world famous.

The first 30 places went to men who seemed to have the best chance of escaping. Most of them could speak German or another European language. They would be given well-tailored clothes, money and railway schedules so that they could travel openly by train. Roger Bushell, Peter Fanshawe and the others in this group had carefully rehearsed their false identities, such as foreign factory owners on their way to visit a branch plant. They would be supplied with forged documents to support those identities.

Wings Day, who had as much escaping experience as any man in the camp, was also in this first group, although he could not speak German. He would pose as an Irish renegade colonel who hated the British, escorted by a "German corporal" who was actually a German-speaking Polish POW.

The rest of the first 100 places were given to men who had made large contributions to the escape, and then the remaining 100 places were drawn from a hat.

Most of these escapers with the higher numbers would be "hard arsers," men who would be roughly dressed, and travelling on foot. They would try to keep to the woods and back roads, avoiding towns. They would have maps, and escape rations, but very little in the way of fake ID. Since they would have to travel hundreds of miles on foot to get out of Germany, these men understood that they had a very slim chance of getting away. At the very least, they could create an uproar. Hank Birkland was among this group, trusting his wits and his endurance to see him through.

Wally's work ensured him a good spot in the tunnel, but he could not speak German or any other European language. He and George Harsh planned to strike out cross-country, perhaps sneaking a ride in box cars as Wally had done before the war. Realistically, Wally knew that he and George didn't have much hope of escaping. But secretly, he hoped they might. After all, the two of them were as tough and resourceful as anybody in the camp.

The Germans sensed that, once again, something was up. Nothing could disguise the air of excitement and purpose in the camp. They knew it, they felt it, but they could not discover where the tunnel was, nor when the breakout was planned. Security was perfect.

There was a thaw toward the end of February, and the penguins went back to dispersing sand outside. One penguin got a little careless, and a couple of guards saw the tell-tale sand sifting out the bottom of his pant legs. They told their sergeant, Herman Glemnitz, what they'd seen.

Now Glemnitz knew for certain that there was still a tunnel underway. But where was it? Who was working on it? That skinny Canadian, Floody! So pale—as if he never saw the sun. Glemnitz had a strong hunch Floody must be involved. And he knew what had to be done.

Chapter 11

THE DARKEST HOUR

The kriegies were lined up in the exercise yard for morning appell. They stamped their feet and thrust their hands into their armpits to keep warm. It was a cold, clear morning at the beginning of March 1944. Wally was impatient to get down into the tunnel for his digging shift. Harry had less than 100 feet to go. They should be ready to break out in two or three weeks.

The guards seemed to be taking longer than usual, double checking their lists and conferring with each other. It was as if they were waiting for something. After about half an hour some senior officers strode into the exercise yard. One of them announced to the assembled prisoners, "When I call your names, come forward." Then he began reading from a list:

"Floody . . . Fanshawe . . . Harsh . . ."

There were over a dozen more names called out, but

Wally was too stunned to register all of them. The chosen men were hustled onto trucks and driven out of the camp. They hadn't even been allowed back into their rooms to gather their few belongings. (These were sent along to them later in the day.) Their destination turned out to be another prison camp called Belaria—smaller and even more tightly guarded than Stalag Luft III. It was only five miles down the road from Stalag Luft III, but that was far enough to dash all of Wally's hopes for escape. He had hacked away at that stinking sand for hundreds of hours, thinking only of the day when he would breathe free air. Now it wasn't going to happen, not for him. He was furious.

Wally never knew how the Germans had selected 20 men for transfer to Belaria. Some of them, including him and Peter Fanshawe, were key members of the X Organization, but others were not. And they had missed Roger Bushell, the leader. Wally always believed that the Germans had simply rounded up men they thought most likely to be involved in escape plans, without hard evidence. His only comfort was that Harry was so well advanced that the tunnellers could carry on without him. From now on, Wally could have no direct part in the escape. He would have to rely on the grapevine of camp life—which included talkative guards, workmen and delivery men who went to both camps, and transferred prisoners—to find out what was going on.

On March 24, Wally awoke to a cold wind that rattled the windows of his hut. Fine, powdery snow was sifting in under the door. He knew that, down the road at Stalag Luft III, Roger Bushell and the other key men in the X Organization had a hard decision to make. This date had been discussed while he was still back in the North Compound as the strongest candidate for escape night. It would be a moonless night, which the escapers needed. It was also a Friday, the best possible night for breakout, because so many extra trains left Sagan on the weekend.

But now the weather had turned bad. The "hard arsers," the men going cross-country on foot, would suffer in the cold and snow. The X Organization could wait for the next moonless period, when the weather would be warmer. But the longer the tunnel existed, the greater the danger that the guards would discover it.

There was another problem that troubled Wally, and he had shared his concern with Roger several weeks ago. The ground above the tunnel was frozen hard now; when warmer weather and spring rains came, he thought there was a risk the tunnel roof might cave in.

Whatever the choice, Wally knew that if the Escape Committee gave the go-ahead, they could not go back on it later in the day. All the travel permits had to be stamped for that night or the next day. It was an all-day job for the forgers. And once it was done, the documents could not be used at a later date.

That night, Wally lay sleepless in his bunk, with only one thought on his mind. What was going on in the North Compound at Stalag Luft III?

* * *

In fact, the X Organization had weighed the risks and come to a decision—the escape would go ahead. As soon as darkness came in the North Compound, men scurried silently from their huts, dodging the restless searchlights. They were dressed as businessmen, work-men and German soldiers—anything but what they were, escaping airmen. By 8:00 p.m., 200 of them were jammed into hut 104. To make room for them, the regu-lar occupants were spending the night in other huts.

The trapdoor under the stove was open, and Harry's electric lights shone up into the hut. At 9:00 p.m., the first escapers made their way down into the tunnel. These were the men with the best chance of getting away, headed for the Sagan train station. Blankets had been laid under the tracks to muffle the sound of the trolleys carrying men down the tunnel. More blankets covered the ground at Piccadilly Circus and at Leicester Square, to keep the escapers' clothes as clean as possible.

Nine-thirty arrived, the scheduled time for men to start breaking out of the tunnel's exit. And then began a string of bad luck.

The wooden exit trap had become swollen with melted snow, and it wouldn't budge. It took 90 minutes of struggle to free it. That was when the escapers discov-ered the second hitch. Despite the best efforts of the tunnel surveyors, the tunnel came up about 25 feet short of the woods. The escapers had to come out at careful intervals, when the coast was clear of patrolling guards.

And then, at 11:30 p.m., air raid sirens began to wail.

A few minutes later, the camp was plunged into darkness. As soon as they spotted the British bombers, the Germans had cut off all electricity in the area. They wanted to be sure there were no lights to guide the planes to their targets.

The tunnel became absolutely black, filled with men packed end to end. Most of them had never been in the tunnel before that night. Even with the lights on, many had found it hard to be below ground in such a small space. Now, in the dark, several men lost their nerve. One man's panicked thrashing started to bring the roof down. He had to be hauled out on the trolley.

Wally's digging partner, Hank Birkland, had been waiting his turn in the tunnel. When he heard what had happened, he crawled through the darkness to the fall and packed the sand back in. Luckily none of the boards had broken, so he was able to jam them back into place.

But more precious time had been lost.

Down the road, Belaria was also blacked out by the air raid. Wally wondered if the escape had gone ahead. If so, he hoped desperately that the escapers were already out of the tunnel and on their way. There was a grim irony to this. His earlier tunnels had been lit by crude oil lamps. The tunnel team had been so proud of Harry's electric lights. On this night, though, the escapers would have been better off with lamps.

When morning finally came, word spread quickly through Belaria. There had been a break from the North Compound at Stalag Luft III. The guards at Belaria were tense and agitated, ordering appells and room searches. And one of them whispered to Wally that 76 men had gotten away. Wally was elated that the escape had gone ahead, but troubled by the number. *Only 76.* Roger had been hoping to take out 200. Wally knew that something must have gone wrong.

Gradually the details trickled over to Belaria. The escape committee had decided that number 87 would have to be the last man out of the tunnel, since dawn was approaching. But just as the 80th man was clambering out, a guard spotted him and fired a wild shot at him. "Don't shoot," the prisoner shouted, *"Nicht shiessen!"* Other guards came running. Three other men were caught in the open, as well as several who were waiting their turns at the bottom of the exit shaft. All of them were thrown into the cooler.

Although the German guards could clearly see where the tunnel ended, none of them felt inclined to go down into it. It took them over an hour to find out which hut the tunnel started in. Meanwhile, they made every prisoner in the camp go outside for an appell. The Germans were desperate to determine exactly how many prisoners had gotten away. When they realized what a large break it was, they were appalled. They knew that they would be punished for it.

As Belaria guards whispered to Wally, the escape was

causing panic all over Germany. All service personnel on leave had been recalled, and every train was being stopped and searched. Every 15 minutes, radio broadcasts warned the public to be on the lookout for the escapees. In all, some 70,000 Germans became involved in the search for the 76 prisoners.

Soon after the escape, the Gestapo arrived at the camp to question the prisoners and search every hut. Colonel von Lindeiner was relieved of his command and, along with some of the guards, was taken away to be court martialled. However, Glemnitz, who had led the search for the tunnels, escaped punishment. He had been transferred to Belaria at the same time Wally was moved there. The Germans filled Harry with sand and plugged the entrance shaft with concrete.

By the end of March, a few recaptured prisoners were being sent back to Stalag Luft III in twos and threes. They were also tossed in the cooler to spend a week or two. So far, this was what the kriegies had expected. Then, in the second week of April, the Senior British Officer in Belaria called a special appell. He had a stunning announcement: the camp commandant had informed him that 50 of the escapers had been shot and killed by the Gestapo. The Gestapo claimed that all of them had been shot "while trying to escape."

Wally and the other kriegies understood that, if the prisoners had offered resistance, some might well have been killed. However, you would expect that others would only be wounded, and survive. Since every one of the 50 had died, Wally and the other kriegies had no doubt that they had simply been murdered. The men of Belaria and Stalag Luft III attached black diamonds to their sleeves as a sign of mourning. Even the German officers and guards in the camps were deeply shocked by the news; one of them quietly told Wally how sorry they were about what had happened.

A few days later, the Germans posted a list of the dead. Roger Bushell, who had organized the escape plan, headed the list. All of these men were Wally's friends. Six of them were Canadians. Wally felt sick when he saw the name of his digging partner, Hank Birkland. And Pat Langford, who had been one of his instructors at Dunnville. Gordon Kidder, another of the Canadians, had gone to school with Wally's wife, Betty. Wings Day was not on the list of the dead, but his whereabouts were unknown. He had gone out of the tunnel and had not been returned to Stalag Luft III. Wally hoped he had been taken to another camp.

The bodies of the 50 men were cremated and urns containing their ashes were eventually returned to Stalag Luft III. On December 4, 1944, a short memorial service was held for the 50 just outside the camp. Some of the Stalag Luft III prisoners had designed and built a memorial to hold the urns. An Anglican minister and a Roman Catholic priest conducted the service, and 30 POW officers were allowed to attend, including Wally and six others from Belaria. Wally laid a wreath on the cairn, and a British bugler from the North Compound played the

*Memorial to the 50 men shot, built by Stalag Luft III
prisoners, just outside the camp.*

lonely notes of the Last Post. Finally, an honour party of
German camp guards fired their guns in salute.

Eventually, the prisoners received small pieces of
good news. Three men had actually succeeded in getting safely away. All three were familiar with the countries they travelled through, and they could speak
German and other European languages. Norwegians
Per Bergsland and Jens Muller took a train across
Germany to the port of Stettin. There they found a ship
that was willing to take them to Sweden, which was a
neutral country during the Second World War. They
reached safety in Stockholm in less than three days. Bob
van der Stok, who was Dutch, took a train to Holland,

but since the Germans occupied his country, he still wasn't safe there. With the help of friends who risked their lives to hide him and transport him, he made his way through Belgium and into France. Finally, after a rugged hike over the Pyrenees, he reached safety in neutral Spain, several months after the escape.

In Belaria, Wally dug no more tunnels. The heavy clay in the camp was unsuitable for them; but that had never stopped him before. He had never been afraid to take chances with his own life in the tunnels, if that could help others to escape. But the odds had changed. Now the prisoners understood that the Germans were prepared to kill them if they tried to escape. Most of the men who had escaped from Stalag Luft III had known they had little real chance of getting home. Their main goal had been to cause a huge disruption in Germany, and they had done that. But the idea had never been to sacrifice their lives.

And there was another reason to stop the escape attempts. Listening to their hidden radios, the prisoners knew that the war could not go on much longer. The long-awaited invasion of Europe had finally come. British and Commonwealth forces and the Americans had landed on the beaches of Normandy, France, on June 6, 1944. Through the summer and fall they were slowly pushing the German forces back toward Germany. Meanwhile, the Russians were winning victories against the Germans in the east. Once again, the prisoners began to hope that they might be home for Christmas.

Chapter 12

THE LONG MARCH

One evening in late January 1945, a kriegie burst into Wally's hut. "This is it!" he said excitedly. "The goons are taking us all out of the camp in half an hour!" Then he dashed off to spread the word.

"They surely picked a fine night for it," George drawled, looking out the frost-etched window. The camp's searchlights lit up the gusts of snowflakes that were swirling around the huts.

Wally was already grabbing the empty Red Cross crates they had used for chairs. "Give me a hand here, George. We've got to make a sled to carry our gear."

All over the camp, the prisoners made frantic preparations. From radio news reports, everyone had known that the Russians were drawing close to Belaria. They had hoped their German guards might simply flee, leaving them behind. Now they knew that the kriegies were to be taken along with them, although no one knew where they were headed.

Wild rumours spread through the camp. They'd be taken to wherever Adolf Hitler was making his last stand, to be traded for better treatment from the victorious allies. Some said they'd be placed around Hitler's headquarters to protect him as human shields. Wally believed there was no point in getting worked up about rumours. In his long years as a prisoner, he had learned that most of them turned out to be untrue. Still, he did have the escapers in the back of his mind. Because of Hitler's anger and humiliation, 50 of them had been shot. How much more furious must Hitler be now, with all his mad dreams collapsing around him?

Wally, George and a Canadian named Kingsley Brown—nicknamed Brownie—worked together to get ready for the march. They mounted their Red Cross crates on two bed-slat runners to make a sturdy sled. Camp blankets, torn into strips and braided, made lines to pull it. They filled the boxes with any food that would keep and wasn't too heavy to carry, such as chocolate bars, cheese and dried fruit. Any other food in the hut was wolfed down. There was no sense rationing it out any more.

The kriegies layered on all their clothes. Wally put newspapers inside his jacket for extra warmth, a trick he'd learned from homeless men when he was riding the rails. The lucky kriegies had mitts and hats, sent by relatives or knitted in the camp. Others made ponchos and hoods out of camp blankets. Few had a decent pair of boots; men stuffed rags or newspapers into the holes in their shoes.

Everyone had a few precious items they couldn't leave behind. For Wally, these included his journal, which he stuffed into his kit bag. He tucked Betty's picture and some of the letters he'd received into the breast pocket of his jacket.

In the end, the German guards weren't ready to move them out until dawn, which was a blessing. The men had needed every extra minute to pull their supplies together.

As the long line of prisoners wound out the gate, guards handed each man a Red Cross parcel from the camp stores. "So *that's* where they've been," Wally said grimly. For the past few months, few Red Cross parcels had arrived for prisoners, and they had suffered constant hunger on German rations.

Wally, George and Brownie added the parcels to the bundles on their sled. The snow was now blowing so strongly that they could only see a few feet ahead. Their eyelashes and beards quickly crusted with ice. They took turns harnessing themselves to the sled and hauling it.

The kriegies had banded together in small groups to help each other—it was the only way to survive. Most had at least a share of a sled where they could place their burdens for part of the march. But some had only their kit bags. Wally saw men throw away supplies, because

Exhausted prisoners rest in the snow during the Long March. This sketch was made by Ley Kenyon, a Stalag Luft III prisoner who took part in the march.

they lacked the strength to carry them any longer. He was so thankful that he and some other prisoners—mostly Canadians—had thought to make sleds.

That night the prisoners were herded into a big, unheated barn. They huddled together for warmth, but nobody got much sleep. Many men were already in bad shape, with frostbitten faces and feet. In the morning, they began to march again. In the afternoon, the wind shifted, bringing a thaw. In some ways, this was worse than the snowfall. As they trudged through dirty slush, their shoes became soaked with water. The soles pulled away from the uppers and flapped with every step. With the snow melting away, the sled got harder and harder to pull. On the third evening, Wally and his friends broke the sled up for firewood. After warming themselves around their small fire, they crawled into a root cellar to sleep.

The roads the kriegies travelled were choked with people and vehicles of all kinds. For the first time, Wally saw the cruel effects of the war on civilians. He saw pathetic, skin-and-bones people dressed in rags. They were from France, Belgium and other countries, and all had been slave labourers for the Germans in Eastern Europe. Now they were struggling westward to try to reach their homes. Wally saw many Germans as well, whole families of refugees, fleeing in terror from the Russian army. There were women and children and old people, with all their remaining possessions piled into carts and wheelbarrows. Everyone on the roads was just trying to stay alive.

The food the prisoners had with them soon ran out. At some of their rest stops, the Germans set up military kitchens to serve them a meal. At others, a farmer might at least provide them with some hot water so that they could make coffee or soup. To Wally's surprise, some Germans who lived along the road came out with food and hot drinks, and gave them to the prisoners limping by. One woman even singled out Canadians to feed, saying that her husband was being treated well in a prisoner-of-war camp in Canada. However, it was never enough, and Wally was always hungry.

The German guards who were with the kriegies didn't have enough to eat either. They were older than their prisoners, and they were exhausted from slogging along beside them. It was easy for the prisoners to slip away from the lines to forage for food. Wally, George and Brownie came upon a group of Frenchmen who had been labourers on a German farm. These men had a whole wagonload of bread. Wally and George traded their wristwatches for three rock-hard loaves.

After a week on the road, the march finally came to an end. Wally and the other prisoners were herded into forty-and-eights, so crowded that many men had to stand. Wally's boxcar was sealed shut and the men had no light. Their only toilet was a box placed in the straw. In the middle of the night, one man began to moan, "I want my mother . . . I want my mother." Wally recognized the voice of this fighter pilot, only 20 years old. He had always been cheerful in captivity, but now he was ill with pneumonia, and he had reached his breaking point. In the dark, Wally climbed over people, making his way down the filthy boxcar. "Let me through," he said. He found the young pilot and calmed him down. "It's okay, boy," Wally said quietly. "We'll get you to your mother soon." The other men in the boxcar with Wally on that sleepless night never forgot his kindness.

When the train finally came to a stop, the prisoners were marched in pouring rain to Luckenwalde, about

35 miles south of the city of Berlin. The prisoner-of-war camp at Luckenwalde was a wretched place. It was packed with thousands of men who had been force-marched there by the retreating Germans, and more were arriving every day. In Wally's compound there were British and Commonwealth and American airmen. Other compounds within the camp held Poles and Frenchmen and Hungarians and Russians.

The barracks were filthy, their walls stained with water and mould. The mattresses stank and were infested with lice, bed bugs and fleas. Wally, along with everyone else, was soon itchy and covered in bites. Although there were stoves in the huts for heat, there were no briquettes or coal to burn in them. Instead, the prisoners made small stoves out of tin cans, and burned scraps of cardboard, twigs and shavings from bed boards in them.

Wally had been undernourished for several years. But this was the first time he thought that he and the other men were in danger of starving. They had eaten everything they had brought from Belaria. No more Red Cross parcels were arriving in the last desperate days of the war. The German guards barely fed them now—a cup of soup at noon and three slices of bread in the evening. There was very little to do and little strength to do it. On February 8, Wally wrote in his journal, "Life is Hell here. Hungry all the time, filthy clothes. I wonder what will happen if the Germans try to move us again—we're in a pretty weak state."

But that never happened. Allied planes passed over the camp day and night, on their way to bomb Berlin. By the beginning of April, the prisoners could hear artillery fire to the east of the camp. And then, one morning, the Germans simply marched out the gates of the camp, leaving the prisoners behind. The next day, April 22, 1945, the Russian Red Army began to arrive, in jeeps, armoured cars and huge tanks. Some prisoners cheered as a Russian tank rolled carefully around the perimeter of the camp, mowing down the wire. But Wally and the other prisoners quickly discovered that they were still not free. Instead, they were caught in a new standoff between the Russians and the Americans.

The American army, invading Germany from the west, and the Russian army, invading Germany from the east, had met at the Elbe River. Now the Americans were camped on the west bank of the Elbe, while Russians controlled the territory east of the river, including the camp at Luckenwalde. The Russians were not ready simply to hand over the prisoners of war they had collected at Luckenwalde. There were anti-Communist Russians who had fought on the German side in the war and who were now in American hands. The Russians wanted to get them back. The Russians wanted to trade them for the Allied air force prisoners at Luckenwalde. This took weeks to negotiate. Wally was forced to spend his 27th birthday still a prisoner.

Outside Luckenwalde, there were still small groups of German soldiers fighting fiercely. As bad as it was inside the camp, most of the unarmed prisoners felt it was better to wait to be turned over to the Americans than to take off on their own. However, the Russians had very little food to share with the prisoners. Even their own troops were expected to forage in the countryside. A group of 10 men, including Wally, was given a truck with a Russian driver and told to go out into the countryside to find some potatoes. Other men were driving cows and sheep into the camp, or coming back with chickens in sacks. By trading or stealing, the Russians and the prisoners managed to stay alive.

The most bitterly disappointing day for Wally was May 8. The day began joyously when the camp woke up to the news that the Germans had surrendered the previous day. The war in Europe was finally over. That afternoon, a convoy of American trucks arrived at the camp, ready to pick up some prisoners. Wally and his friends began to run toward the trucks, but the Russians fired machine guns over their heads to stop them. The American trucks were forced to withdraw.

Finally, toward the end of May 1945, a deal was struck. A convoy of Russian trucks took Wally and other Allied airmen to the Elbe river. The original bridge had been destroyed in the fierce fighting at the end of the war, but the Americans had placed a pontoon bridge across the water. Wally, George and Brownie scrambled across it. When Wally stepped down from the bridge, he turned to his friends and said simply, "By God . . . we made it."

Wally at the time of his release from Luckenwalde (Stalag Luft IIIA). He is wearing a Yugoslavian hat, an Afrika Korps jacket (German army) and American pants and boots.

Chapter 13

COMING HOME

"Jeez, look at those guys!" one young American soldier said to another. "They're eating the bread like it's cake." He was talking about the blissful expressions on the faces of Wally and the other released prisoners as they savoured each morsel of soft, white bread. The Americans had no way of knowing how long it had been since the kriegies had experienced this simple pleasure. For the first time in years, they had all the food they could eat.

The Americans had taken over what used to be a big Luftwaffe base. There they welcomed the former prisoners of war from Luckenwalde with hot showers, clean clothes and delicious food—all of it free of charge. In a couple of days, they assured Wally, a plane would be taking him back to England. He could start to think about going home.

On May 30, 1945, Betty got a telegram informing her that Wally had been liberated. Once he reached England, it took a little time for him to be sent home to Canada, but he finally arrived on July 1, 1945.

Like thousands of other veterans, Wally set about putting his life back together. When the war began in 1939, he had been 21 years old. Now he was 27. He knew he didn't want to stay in the air force, but he had to figure out what he could do in peacetime. At first, it seemed to make sense to use his flight training. With a friend named Herb May, he operated a chartered air service from Toronto's island airport. His airline flew business executives to Yellowknife and other northern mining areas. His planes also did the flying sequences for a feature film set in Canada, called *Bush Pilot*. By the time the film came out (and quickly vanished), he'd had enough of flying and closed down the business.

On September 30, 1946, Betty and Wally's first son, Brian, was born. Two days later, Wally received news that he had been awarded the Order of the British Empire by King George VI. The text of the award said, in part,

> Flight Lieutenant Floody made a very thorough study of tunnelling work and devised many different methods and techniques. He became one of the leading organizers and indefatigable workers in the tunnels themselves. Besides being arduous, his work was frequently dangerous. . . .

Flight Lieutenant Floody was buried under heavy falls of sand. . . . It was only due to extraordinary luck and presence of mind of his helpers that he was rescued alive. . . . Time and time again, projects were started and discovered by the Germans, but, despite all dangers and difficulties, Flight Lieutenant Floody persisted, showing a marked degree of courage and devotion to duty.

The story of the courageous prisoner of war with the OBE *and* a new baby made all the Toronto newspapers. Betty, still in hospital with her son, chatted happily with the reporters. But Wally was reluctant to talk to them. "Things are kind of piling up on me" was the only quote the *Toronto Star* got. Wally flatly refused to go to London to receive his medal from the king. He felt that he was no hero; that he had only done his duty. Fifty men had been murdered after going through the tunnel he built; he did not want an award for his part in that. That is when Betty began to understand what a heavy weight Wally was carrying around.

In 1947, Wally got a job in London and the Floodys moved to England. Their second child, Richard, was born during the two years they lived there. Wally was happy to reconnect with his RAF friend Wings Day. Wings was lucky to be alive. When he and several other escapers were recaptured, they were thrown into Sachsenhausen, a German concentration camp. Here the

Nazis were murdering thousands of Jews, as well as Communists, trade union leaders and others who opposed their regime. Wings would never forget the horrors he saw there. He and the other prisoners of war were kept in a separate section and better treated. However, after Wings escaped yet again and was recaptured, he was sentenced to death. The war ended before the sentence could be carried out.

Wally and Wings discussed the upcoming trials of the men who had murdered the Stalag Luft III escapers. Wally had thought, with the enormous crimes against humanity that were under investigation after the war, the murderers of 50 air force officers would never be brought to justice. And yet it was happening.

In June 1944, British Foreign Minister Anthony Eden had assured Parliament that "His Majesty's government . . . are firmly resolved that these foul criminals shall be tracked down. They will be brought to exemplary justice." As soon as the war ended in 1945, the RAF's Special Investigations Branch—made up of five officers and 14 non-commissioned officers—travelled to Germany and began its investigations.

They learned that the orders for the murders had come directly from Adolf Hitler. He had flown into a rage when he learned that 76 airmen had escaped. At first, he demanded that all of the escapers be shot. His advisors persuaded him that it would be better to keep some alive. Then, if they claimed that the men were shot while escaping, they might be believed. Finally, Hitler agreed to 50—roughly two out of three.

Hitler had committed suicide during the last days of the war. He could not be prosecuted for any of his war crimes, which had caused the deaths of millions of people. But the Gestapo officers who had carried out Hitler's orders and murdered the Stalag Luft III escapers *were* alive, and the Royal Air Force was determined to find them.

It seemed an impossible task. In the rubble and confusion of Germany right after the war, there were millions of refugees, moving from place to place. How could they find a handful of guilty men, eager to hide their identities? The RAF investigators had some help from the U.S. War Crimes Liaison and other groups investigating war crimes. But above all, they simply would not give up. They questioned more than 60,000 people and slowly built a case against 72 Gestapo agents who had worked in 13 different Gestapo offices.

The first trials of some of these men were held in Hamburg, Germany, in 1947. Eventually 21 of them were executed, and 17 received long prison sentences. Most of the others were believed to be dead: some had been killed in Allied air raids near the end of the war, and some had committed suicide. Only one man stayed free in East Germany until his death many years later.

The last man to be brought to justice went on trial in 1968. He was sentenced to two years in prison.

Painful details about the last hours of Wally's friends came out during the trials. After the escapers were captured, they were held in local jails wherever they were caught. Then Gestapo agents came and took some of them away by car. These prisoners believed they were being taken back to Stalag Luft III. They expected nothing worse than a spell in the cooler. Singly or in groups of two or three, they were driven to remote spots. The cars pulled over, and they were told to get out and stretch their legs since it would be a long journey. Then they were shot in the back of the head. It was terrible, but at least now Wally knew.

In 1951, Paul Brickhill, an Australian who had been imprisoned at Stalag Luft III, wrote a best-selling book called *The Great Escape*. From then on, the Stalag Luft III breakout of March 1944 was always known by this name. The book contained many admiring references to Wally Floody's tunnelling work and bravery. Once again, reporters wrote stories about him. Because of his unusual name, he was never difficult to track down. But once again, the newspaper stories had no quotations from Wally himself—he still wasn't ready to talk about what had happened.

In the mid–1950s, Wally finally found work that interested him and suited his outgoing personality. He set up his own business as a trade association manager. His clients included trade associations for florists and soft drink manufacturers, and Canada's food brokers association. Wally's job involved coming up with new

Wally with Betty and their two sons,
Brian and Richard, around 1963.

ways for these organizations to promote their products. He also coordinated their national conventions, and he did a lot of public speaking on his clients' behalf.

Wally's job included a great deal of travel, which he enjoyed. Wherever he went, he was welcome in the homes of ex-kriegies. He was one of the founders of the RCAF's Ex-Prisoner of War Association and became one of its best-known figures. The association focused on two things: keeping alive the bond of friendship the kriegies had formed during the war, and helping ex-prisoners who were in need. But they also became involved in community volunteer work.

Wally's Toronto chapter of the Ex-POW Association worked for many years with the Canadian Cancer Society. Wally, with his connections in the floral business, would arrange for one million fresh daffodils to be shipped from Victoria, B.C., for the Cancer Society's fundraising sales in Toronto. Remembering how important Red Cross parcels had been to hungry kriegies, Wally also worked as a volunteer for the Red Cross. He set up Boxing Day blood donor clinics in Toronto hotels. To entice people to give blood on a holiday, he arranged for celebrities to visit the clinics and entertain.

Wally always knew he was one of the lucky ones. During the Second World War, about 12,500 Canadian airmen had been killed. About 2,300 had become prisoners of war, and not all of them made it home, either. Wally would always say, "For me, every day of living is a bonus."

Chapter 14

BACK TO GERMANY

One day early in 1962, Wally got an unexpected phone call.

"Hello, my name is John Sturges," said the caller. "I'm planning to make a movie about the Great Escape. I wonder if you'd be interested in being my technical advisor?"

Wally was cautious. He'd seen too many war movies with cartoonish heroics. He didn't want to be involved with anything like that. Sturges reassured him that he wanted to make every detail of life in Stalag Luft III as accurate as possible. That's why he wanted the help of a man who had actually been there.

"I'd have to see the script first," Wally said.

"No problem," Sturges replied.

Soon Wally had a rough draft of the script in his hands. The story began with the most troublesome air force escapers arriving at Stalag Luft III, the brand new "escape-proof" camp. Within hours the X Organization began planning a breakout. A man named Roger Bartlett—very much like Roger Bushell—was in charge as "Big X." The script worked its way through all the events Wally remembered so well: choosing the sites for the three tunnels, bribing the guards, forging the documents, hiding the sand, and above all, digging the tunnels and scrambling out when they collapsed.

Wally chuckled when he came to the scene where a character called Cavendish swings himself into his upper bunk, only to fall right through it. Wally had seen this happen to an airman after half his bed boards had been taken to shore up the tunnel. Americans played a bigger role in the script than they had in the actual escape. No Americans had gone out in the real tunnel because they had all been moved to another compound months before the breakout. The only Canadian in the script had a very small part. But Wally understood that the film was being made by an American studio and that their audiences wanted to see American stars in lead roles.

All the terms the kriegies had used were there: "goons," "ferrets" and "stooges." However, Wally noticed right away that the slang was wrong. The characters sometimes sounded like young men of the 1960s, not the 1940s. Maybe he could do something about that.

In the meantime, Wally had talked again with John

Sturges and learned more about him. Sturges was a well-known Hollywood director who had made many action movies. He'd been trying for over 10 years to get a movie studio interested in making a movie about the escape from Stalag Luft III. They'd shown little enthusiasm. As one said, "There's—what—76 guys trying to escape and only three get away? Who'd want to see something depressing like that?" Then in 1961, Sturges directed a western called *The Magnificent Seven*. It became a big hit. After that, the Mirisch production company was happy to provide $4 million— enough to make a large-scale action film in 1962—for *The Great Escape*.

Wally was impressed by Sturges' commitment to the project. The director explained that he had wanted to shoot the movie at the site of the real camp near Sagan. But Sagan was now inside the borders of Poland, and Poland was controlled by the Soviet Union. In the 1960s, the Soviet Union was locked in a "Cold War" of suspicion and competition with the United States. Hollywood film crews were not welcome there. Instead, they were making the movie in southern Germany, in Geiselgasteig, near Munich.

Sturges told Wally that a British actor named Richard Attenborough would be playing Roger Bartlett. Two American actors that Wally knew from television would play the other leads: James Garner would be Bob Hendley, the scrounger, and Steve McQueen would play scrappy Virgil Hilts. Wally was looking forward to

On the set of The Great Escape: *Wally in the middle, James Garner on the left and Steve McQueen on the right.*

meeting Charles Bronson, who would play the "Tunnel King." In the movie, he would be a Polish airman named Danny who battled claustrophobia. This was a fear that had never troubled Wally, but he could see that it would make the film more dramatic.

On May 24, 1962, Wally Floody flew from Toronto to Germany. The next day, Sturges drove him to the set of the film, where construction was almost finished.

It was a grey day, and very cold for May. Wind and rain whipped Wally's hair as he got out of the car. His shoes squelched in the mud as he walked through the gate. He had been expecting to see simple false-front sets. He had imagined walking behind them and seeing the support beams that held them up. Instead, he felt as if he'd stepped back in time.

There was the barbed-wire fence with the guard towers at each corner. Ahead of him were the huts, arranged in neat rows. They smelled of fresh lumber, just as they had when he arrived at Stalag Luft III, more than seventeen years before. Then two German soldiers appeared, marching briskly toward him. Wally froze for a minute. "Welcome to Germany, Mr. Floody," said one of them with a broad smile. They were two extras from the movie, ready to appear in some publicity pictures. Wally smiled gamely as the two "guards" pretended to seize and handcuff him for the photographer.

Wally had brought Betty with him to Germany. She first saw the film set a couple of days after their wedding anniversary. Wally had never liked to talk about his war experiences. But when Betty saw the barracks and the barbed wire, it gave her some idea of what her husband had been through. They had thought they might have time for some sightseeing on their trip. However, over the next two weeks, Wally put in 12-hour workdays.

Everyone working on the film wanted his advice. "Is this how the air pump worked?" a man from the prop department asked. "Not quite," said Wally, and he showed him how it should be changed. He pointed out to the costume department that the prisoners' uniforms should be shabby and mismatched. The art department asked him to take a look at the forged documents they would give the escapers. Did they look like the ones the prisoners had created in the camp? Richard Attenborough wanted to talk to him about what the real Roger Bushell was like. Charles Bronson, who had once been a coal miner, wanted to share underground experiences with Wally.

Above all, Wally was curious to see how the filmmakers would recreate the escape tunnel, Harry. He

On the set, Wally (left) is examining the track system for the tunnel, along with assitant property manager Paul Pollard (in cap) and prop master William Agnone.

knew that the filmmakers wanted him to examine it closely. To his relief, Wally learned that he would not have to go underground. The movie's tunnel would be above ground and indoors. John Sturges took him to an enormous movie soundstage, which to Wally looked a lot like an airplane hangar. This was where all the interior scenes of the movie would be shot. The tunnel set ran the full length of the soundstage, about level with Wally's knees. It had a floor, a roof and a back wall, but it was open on the fourth side. Beside the tunnel was a length of track along which the large, heavy movie camera could glide. When one of the characters rolled down the tunnel on the trolley, the camera could keep pace with him.

The film's production designer, Fernando Carrere, asked Wally to climb inside the tunnel and move around. Was it too big? Wally, no longer the gaunt prisoner of war, decided that even with the extra pounds he had put on over the years he was still a little too comfortable in the tunnel. He suggested that they should move the ceiling down a little.

Before returning to Canada, Wally had dinner with some of the people he had advised. "Let me tell you something," he said. "I know that you're getting everything right, because I had terrible nightmares last night."

Chapter 15

THE GREAT ESCAPE ON THE BIG SCREEN

Wally had never seen a complete script for the film. There wasn't one, even though six screenwriters had worked on it. No one had ever solved the problem of what would happen after the prisoners broke out of the camp. John Sturges, an experienced director of action films, wasn't too worried. He felt that some of the best action sequences could only be planned when a film's crew and cast were actually on location. He also had some writers with him in Germany who could sketch out a scene quickly. But he wasn't expecting the difficulties he would have with Steve McQueen.

On their first trip to Germany, Betty and Wally had been charmed by James Garner and several of the other actors, who were friendly and relaxed. But Steve McQueen was another story. He seemed tense and unhappy. He wasn't yet the big star he would become, and he was very insecure. One day, the film's publicist wanted to take pictures of McQueen walking beside Wally on the set. McQueen made sure that he walked on a raised ridge of earth, so that he wouldn't look so short. More seriously, McQueen worried that his part was not as good as James Garner's, and that Garner was going to "steal the picture" from him. Soon after Wally returned to Canada, McQueen walked off the set. He

On the set of The Great Escape: *Wally (in suit and tie) watching a scene being filmed with James Garner. The director, John Sturges, is wearing sunglasses and is seated beside Wally.*

said that he would not come back until the script was changed to make his character more exciting.

When Wally made his second trip to Germany to watch some of the filming, he found out how Sturges had persuaded McQueen to return. McQueen's character, Virgil Hilts, was now going to make his getaway on a stolen motorcycle. The chase would end in a spectacular 60-foot jump over a barbed-wire fence. McQueen was, in real life, an excellent motorcyclist who often raced in his spare time. In the end, though, one of his friends performed the jump, because the filmmakers refused to let McQueen take the risk.

Wally understood that the film had to be thrilling, but he was a little worried. How would former prisoners of war react to these Hollywood heroics? Would they understand that, as the film's technical advisor, he had no control over such things?

He had to wait a year to find out.

In the spring of 1963, the film's producers sent Wally on a trip around North America to create interest in the film before it was released. Everywhere he went, reporters wrote admiring stories about the "ex-cowboy, ex-miner, ex–Spitfire pilot" who had tried to tunnel out of a prisoner-of-war camp. Over and over, Wally told how the tunnels were dug, how the sand was dispersed and how he missed his chance to escape. He talked about the desire for freedom that had fuelled everyone's efforts. And he made sure no one who interviewed him forgot that 50 men—many of them his friends—had been murdered by the Gestapo.

The Canadian premiere of *The Great Escape* was to be held at the Odeon theatre in Toronto. Wally made sure that many former kriegies received invitations. He also arranged for the screening to be a fundraiser to benefit the RCAF Ex-Prisoner of War Association's Benevolent Fund. The fund helped to take care of former prisoners of war who were in need. In 1963, for instance, they were helping out with the medical expenses of a Hamilton, Ontario, man who had suffered brain damage in a wartime parachute jump. They also paid travel expenses so that the man's parents could come from the Maritimes to visit him.

On the evening of July 3, 1963, an RCAF band marched along Carleton Street to the Odeon theatre, playing bagpipes. As cameras flashed, Wally, dressed in a white dinner jacket, and Betty, glamorous in a satin evening dress, arrived at the theatre with the Lieutenant Governor of Ontario.

Then the audience took their seats, the lights went down, and a stirring march tune filled the theatre. On the screen, German trucks rumbled down the road, taking prisoners to the new "escape-proof" camp. It was an odd experience for Wally to see finished scenes that had looked so different when he was on the movie set. He was struck by how realistic the tunnel seemed.

It looked cramped and dirty and dangerous, just like the ones he dug in Stalag Luft III. Wally couldn't help glancing at the faces of his ex-kriegie friends to see how they were taking the movie. To his relief, they seemed completely caught up in the story. They laughed when McQueen's character, Hilts, first hears about the escape plan from Big X and exclaims, "Two hundred and fifty guys—just walkin' down the road? You're crazy! You oughta be locked up!" (Actually, Wally had never heard Roger talk about more than 200, but that was Hollywood for you.) The ex-kriegies were quiet and intent during the serious scenes. At the end, along with the rest of the audience, they cheered, whistled and clapped enthusiastically.

At the party after the screening, a reporter approached Wally to ask him what he thought of the film. "I felt a little nervous until my fellow kriegies had a chance to see it," he admitted. "But now they've okayed it—100 per cent." The next day came the best news of all: the premiere had raised $10,000 for the RCAF Ex-Prisoner of War Association.

It had taken Wally many years to be comfortable speaking publicly about his experiences as a prisoner of war. From now on, he accepted his role as one of the public faces for the Stalag Luft III escape, especially in Canada.

The Great Escape was a big hit during the summer of 1963, and it has been a popular movie ever since. In 2003, the American Film Institute placed it high on its list of the 50 most thrilling films in movie history. The 40-year-old movie has kept pace with the times, released first on video and then on DVD, and even turned into a video game. As the years went by, Wally remained pleased that he had agreed to advise the film-makers. Even though the movie changed or exaggerated some events, especially those that occurred after the breakout, it helped to keep alive the memory of the Stalag Luft III escapers. "It was a fictional account of a factual event," he would explain patiently to inter-viewers, "but all the technical details were as accurate as possible."

Chapter 16

LIVING HISTORY

A CBC reporter once asked Wally Floody, "After the movie came out, were you treated in a different way, were you treated more as a hero?"

Wally laughed. "Oh, I don't really think so," he said. "I've got two boys and when the movie had been out for about two years, they came into the house one day saying, 'Mother, is it true that Daddy was once a cowboy?'—They couldn't have cared less about the Great Escape."

But the truth was, Wally Floody was linked with the Great Escape for the rest of his life. On the anniversary of the March 1944 escape and on Remembrance Day, newspaper and television reporters would come calling. They'd want Wally to tell them the story of the tunnels once again.

Reporters often asked him what he thought might

have happened if he had taken part in the escape. This was a question Wally had asked himself many times over the years. "Do you think you would have been one of the lucky ones?" one young journalist inquired.

"Well, of course everybody thinks that," Wally replied. "But I did spend some time riding the freight trains, and I had been a miner in Northern Ontario. I had probably had more experience in hard living than quite a few of the other men. But who knows? There's a lot of luck, you know." He paused and added quietly, "I've said to my wife I might have been home earlier and she says, 'yes, and you might have been dead,' so there you are."

Betty filled scrapbooks with newspaper clippings about her husband, and she collected a boxful of video-taped interviews. Yet, no matter how many times he had to answer the same questions over the years, Wally responded with courtesy and good humour. He especially liked to visit schools, including a visit to his own former high school, Northern Secondary.

In his private life, too, his wartime experiences remained important. Most of his closest friends were former prisoners of war. They held reunions every few years, in various parts of Canada, in the United States, and in England. In August 1970, their Toronto reunion was front page news because of the special guest they had invited: Herman Glemnitz, now 71 years old, and once a German security guard at Stalag Luft III.

As news cameras flashed, Glemnitz shook hands

The POW reunion held at the Royal York Hotel in Toronto in August 1970. From left: Herman Glemnitz, Wally and Harry "Wings" Day.

with Wally and Wings Day. Then, for the benefit of reporters, Wally and Glemnitz kidded each other. "I didn't know anything about any tunnels," Wally said to his former guard with a grin.

"Oh, come on, Floody," Glemnitz laughed, "I can't put you in the cooler now. You can tell us all about them."

Wally and Betty had always kept in touch with George Harsh, and visited him yearly at his home in New Jersey. Shortly after his wife died, George had a stroke. He had no family or friends in the States to look after him. Wally and Betty moved him to Toronto, where they cared for him in their own home. Wally also made sure that other ex-kriegies visited often, so that George wouldn't be lonely. George died peacefully in January 1980.

Near the end of his own life, Wally suffered from chronic lung disease. He was a non-smoker, and his family believed that his problems had started with the grit and sand he inhaled in the many tunnels he dug. Nevertheless, he tried to stay active. He appeared at the Canadian National Exhibition in Toronto in 1987, with a model of a Great Escape tunnel. It had been built by students at Danforth Technical School under his supervision. For three days, Wally stood beside the display and explained to passersby how the tunnel was built and used. In the summer of 1989, he travelled to Ottawa for his last ex-prisoner-of-war reunion. He lugged a portable oxygen tank with him, and got around in a special scooter. If anyone tried to sympathize with him, he simply said, "Well, it's a damn sight better than being dead!"

Wally Floody died in his sleep on September 25, 1989. At the time of his death, he had been arranging to purchase a special van that his scooter could drive right into. He'd hoped to attend just one more reunion, scheduled for the spring of 1990.

Shortly before he died, Wally had been talking to Betty yet again about the men who had been shot after escaping from Stalag Luft III through the tunnel he

Wally in about 1987.

had engineered. "Those boys had no funerals," he said, "and I don't want one either." Betty honoured his wish, but a few days after his death, she and her sons had a gathering for all the people who loved and respected Wally Floody. Kingsley Brown—who had shared the Long March with Wally at the end of the war—wrote from Nova Scotia of a friend who "was an unflagging reminder that no matter how hard the going, life was good and well worth living." Paul Brickhill's message from Australia praised Wally as "one of the gutsiest guys I ever knew."

Just as she had carefully saved all the other stories that appeared since she'd met Wally, Betty gathered the messages and the obituaries that appeared in newspapers across Canada, and in the *Times* of London, and placed them in her scrapbook. They contained many words to cherish.

"Wally was living Canadian history," one veteran was quoted as saying. "He always kept on fighting, and other men took inspiration from that."

HISTORICAL NOTE

Prisoners of War

During the Second World War, almost 10,000 Canadians became prisoners of war. More than 7,000 were in the army and more than 2,500 were in the air force. Fewer than 100 men from the Royal Canadian Navy became prisoners of war.

By far the largest number of Canadian prisoners—more than 7,000—were held by the Germans. Germany had signed the Geneva Convention in 1929. This international agreement laid out how prisoners of war should be treated. For instance, their quarters had to be heated, and they were to be fed as well as the capturing country's troops. If prisoners tried to escape, their punishment was to be no more severe than a period of solitary confinement (being put in a cell by themselves). Prisoners were usually held at camps run by the service from which they came. For instance,

Allied airmen were held in camps run by the Luftwaffe, the German air force. These camps were entirely separate from the concentration camps—slave labour and death camps—run by the Nazi *Schutzstaffel* or SS. In the concentration camps, millions of Jews were murdered, as well as gypsies, Poles and many other groups targeted by the Nazis.

For most of the war, the Germans treated the majority of their prisoners of war from Britain, the Commonwealth and the United States reasonably well, although there were differences among camps. Air force prisoners tended to be better treated than army prisoners, and officers were often treated better than non-officers. Russia had not signed the Geneva Convention, and the Germans used this as an excuse to treat their Russian prisoners harshly, barely feeding them and using them as slave labourers.

Meanwhile, Britain had asked Canada to set up prison camps for German prisoners of war. Most of them were Luftwaffe airmen who had been shot down over England. Canada agreed, and established prison camps across the country. The two largest camps, holding about 12,000 prisoners of war each, were near Lethbridge and Medicine Hat, Alberta. These prisoners, far from combat zones and wartime shortages, were well fed and humanely treated. They were repatriated (sent back home) at the end of the war.

Japan had also signed the Geneva Convention in 1929, but its government had not ratified (approved) it, so Japan did not follow Convention standards for prisoners during World War II. The Japanese military at that time believed that a soldier should fight to the death. Surrender was unthinkable. They viewed their prisoners of war with contempt and treated them harshly. About 1,700 Canadians were held by the Japanese; some 1,680 of them were captured in a single day, when Hong Kong fell on December 25, 1941. About 300 of these prisoners—18 per cent of the total—died during the war. Many others had severe and lasting health problems, caused by near-starvation and untreated illnesses and injuries during their captivity.

GLOSSARY

Allies: Led by Britain (and the Commonwealth countries), the U.S.S.R. and the United States, the Allies were the countries that fought against Germany, Italy and Japan during World War II

Appell: Roll call in a German POW camp

Axis: The Axis was made up of the countries that fought against the Allies during World War II. These included Germany, Italy and later Japan.

Big X: The code name for Roger Bushell during the planning of the Great Escape

The British Commonwealth Air Training Plan (BCATP): This program prepared some 130,000

aircrew to serve in World War II. Most of the training took place in Canada.

Dulag Luft (short for *Durchgangslager Luftwaffe*): A transit camp for air force prisoners

Elementary Flying Training School (EFTS): A BCATP school that gave future pilots basic flying training

Ferrets: Kriegie slang for the guards who specialized in uncovering escape plans, especially tunnels under construction

Gestapo (*Geheime Staatspolizei*): The state security police of Nazi Germany

Goons: Kriegie slang for the German guards in a prisoner-of-war camp

Initial Training School (ITS): A BCATP school that determined which aircrew designation (pilot, navigator, etc.) each recruit was best suited to become

Kriegie: What an Allied POW in German camps called himself; short for the German word *Kriegsgefangener* (plural *Kriegsgefangenen*), meaning "prisoner of war"

Luftwaffe: The German air force in World War II

Manning Depot: A place that introduced men to Royal Canadian Air Force training while they waited for room in an Initial Training School

Messerschmitt: A type of German fighter plane

Operational Training Unit (OTU): The final step in the BCATP, allowing airmen to prepare for combat flying. Most BCATP graduates received their OTU training in Britain.

Penguins: Kriegie slang for the men who secretly carried sand away from the escape tunnels

POW: Prisoner of war

RAF: The Royal Air Force, Britain's air force

RCAF: The Royal Canadian Air Force

Red Cross: The International Committee of the Red Cross was founded in Switzerland in 1863. Its original goal was to take care of soldiers wounded in wartime. Many nations responded by setting up their own Red Cross organizations, including Canada in 1896. During World War II, the Canadian Red Cross co-ordinated $80 million in money and materials to aid sick or wounded service people, as well as prisoners of war.

Rhubarb: A low-level attack on ground targets by a small number of fighter planes

Service Flying Training School (SFTS): A BCATP school where pilots learned advanced flying techniques such as night and instrument flying

Squadron: The basic Allied air force flying unit of 24 planes

Stalag Luft: Short for *Stammlager Luftwaffe*, meaning "a prisoner-of-war camp for airmen"

Stooges: Kriegie slang for the prisoners who tracked the movements of German guards

Supermarine Spitfire: A British-made fighter plane

Sweeps: Large-scale Allied fighter plane operations, called "circuses" if the fighters were escorting bombers or "rodeos" if only fighter planes were involved

U-boats: *Unterseeboots*, meaning "undersea boats"; German submarines

ACKNOWLEDGEMENTS

First of all, I want to thank Brian Floody, Wally's son, and Catherine Heron, Wally's sister, for generously sharing with me family photos, journals and scrapbooks, as well as their vivid memories. My husband, Eric Zweig, tirelessly tracked down details of Wally's early sports and mining careers. Retired Lieutenant General A.P. "Bub" Clark of the United States Air Force shared his memories of Wally at Stalag Luft III. Retired Wing Commander Donald Laidler, RCAF, who was a BCATP instructor, and his son, retired Lieutenant Colonel John Laidler, Canadian Forces, reviewed the air force chapters. I also received valuable help from the following people: Dan Diamond, Linda Cobon, Canadian National Exhibition Archives; Jodi Ann Eskritt, Curator, RCAF Memorial Museum, Trenton, Ontario; Duane J. Reed, Archivist, USAF Academy Library, Colorado Springs,

ACKNOWLEDGEMENTS

Colorado; Professor Jonathan Vance, University of Western Ontario, London, Ontario; Bryce Day, Chief Librarian, Teck Centennial Library, Kirkland Lake, Ontario; Robin Ormerod, Director/Curator, and Lynda Sinclair, Museum of Northern History at the Sir Harry Oakes Chateau, Kirkland Lake, Ontario; and John Laverty, Head, Northern Secondary School Library, Toronto, Ontario. Don Sedgwick, my agent, has encouraged me and smoothed my path on many projects, including this one, and Lynne Missen of HarperCollins was the attentive, thoughtful editor all authors hope to find.

PICTURE CREDITS

PICTURE CREDITS

Nicholas Morant/National Archives of Canada (PA 140659), for the photo on page 25.

Mrs. J. Barnett, for the illustration by Ley Kenyon on page 101, and for the illustrations on pages 57, 59, 61, which were redrawn by William Band.

The Globe and Mail, for the photo on page 131.

The Red Cross, for the map of Germany and surrounding areas, which was modified, on pages *viii* and *ix*.